MW00862053

THE SIX-DAY
BICYCLE RACES

THE SIX-DAY BICYCLE RACES

PETER JOFFRE NYE

with Jeff Groman

and Mark Tyson

Van der Plas Publications/

Cycle Publishing, San Francisco

Copyright © 2006, Peter Joffre Nye
Printed in Hong Kong

Van der Plas Publications/Cycle Publishing
1282 7th Avenue
San Francisco, CA 94122, USA
Website: http://www.cyclepublishing.com
E-mail: con.tact@cyclepublishing.com

Distributed or represented to the book trade by:
USA: Midpoint Trade Books, Kansas City, KS
UK: Orca Book Services/Chris Lloyd Sales and Marketing Services, Poole, Dorset
Australia: Tower Books, Frenchs Forest, NSW

Cover and interior design: Yvo Riezebos/Hatty Lee
Frontispiece photo: The two-rider team format introduced into New York City's Madison Square Garden has been called "Madison" ever since.

Publisher's Cataloging in Publication Data
Nye, Peter Joffre, 1947–
The Six-Day Bicycle Races: America's Jazz-Age Sport.
Bibliography: P. 28 cm. Includes index.
1. Bicycles and bicycling
I. Title: America's Jazz-Age Sport
II. Authorship: Groman, Jeff; Tyson, Mark
Library of Congress Control Number: 2005937317
ISBN 1-892495-49-X/978-1-892495-49-5, Hardcover

To Devin and Els Heyne-Groman, Claire

and Noreen Landis-Tyson & Valerie Elaine

Nye, who gave us the blue sky to rescue

the history of this once robust sport.

TABLE OF CONTENTS

1. An American Sports Tradition 9

2. The Early Days 23

3. Bobby Walthour, Sr. 33

4. Two Promoters: John M. Chapman & Tex Rickard 43

5. Floyd MacFarland 49

6. The Points System, 1916 61

7. The Roaring Twenties 67

8. Reggie McNamara, Part I 77

9. Crashes, Trainers, and Drugs 83

10. Mechanics 95

11. Track Construction 101

12. According to Damon Runyon & James Thurber... 107

13. Feeding Frenzy 113

14. Bobby Walthour, Jr. 121

15. Jimmy Walthour, Jr. 131

16. Cycling Czar 137

17. Willie and the Outlaws, Part I 143

18. The Twenties Ended "with a Whimper" 147

19. Willie and the Outlaws, Part II 163

20. Harry Mendel 171

21. Gustav Kilian & Heinz Vopel 177

22. Reggie McNamara, Part II 181

23. Fade to Dark 185

24. Post-War Recovery 193

25. Last Hurrah 201

26. Exported to Europe 207

Acknowledgements 214

Author and contributor bios 215

Bibliography 216

Index 221

6-DAY BIKE RACE

OFFICIAL
15¢
PROGRAM

55th
INTERNATIONAL
6-DAY BIKE RACE
Nov. 26 to Dec. 2, 1933

AN AMERICAN SPORTS TRADITION

Bicycle racers were America's superstars of the Roaring Twenties. While major league baseball was big in 1919, it got knocked from the limelight the next year because of the lurid headline coverage generated by the World Series "Black Sox" scandal.

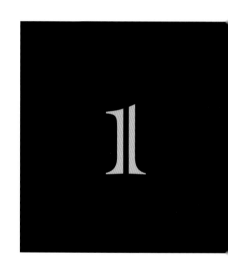

Although there were eleven professional football teams that would form the National Football League, their franchises went on sale in 1920 in Canton, Ohio, for $100 each. As for basketball, it was only a college sport. Where was the money in sports then? It was the bicycle racers who pulled in the big bucks.

At a time when the printed word ruled in the media, newspapers published several editions daily with coverage devoted to the Six-Day bicycle races—the original multi-day physical contest, six days and nights straight, with plenty of action. Riders in vibrant-colored silk jerseys hunched over steel frames and wooden-rimmed wheels that had no brakes and only one gear.

Paul Gallico, a *New York Daily News* reporter later celebrated as author of *The Poseidon Adventure*, informed his readers: "And this marrrrrrvelous contest of skill, endurance, strength, ignorance, speed and stamina is yours to view for a trifling sum laid down at the box office, a few coins of the realm, ladeeeeeez and gen'lemen. See the athletes eat fourteen meals a day. See the man fall off his wheel and tear his pants."

New York City's Madison Square Garden held the Super Bowl of Sixes. *The New York Times* reported in March 1921, "Men and women enthusiasts, thrilled by the spectacle of the cyclists tearing around the pine saucer at breakneck speed, yelled themselves hoarse in a din which transformed the Garden into bedlam."

In the summers, track riders competed in sprints and races over various distances on outdoor board tracks. During the winter indoor season, they strove for fame and fortune in Six-Day races on shorter, more steeply banked wooden indoor ovals—measuring ten laps to the mile, or 176 yards.

Between November and March, Six-Day racers commuted by train on their circuit to Chicago, Boston, Buffalo, Toronto, St. Louis, Indianapolis, Des Moines, Minneapolis, San Francisco, Los Angeles, Atlanta, and other cities. There were as many Sixes in North America as in all of Europe.

Fifteen teams of two men each competed. One rider maintained the team's place, while his partner left the human squirrel cage to eat, nap or answer nature's call. The riders of each team wore identical jerseys, always nationalistic to entice patriotic immigrants, even if the team in the green-white-and-red of Italy had only one Italian and his partner was a U.S. cyclist of Italian heritage or came from Australia or Canada.

Teams rode more than 2,500 miles—farther than the Tour de France, which lasts three weeks.

In Six-Day races, the launch of a rider suddenly shooting from the rolling pack to "steal" a lap set off a chase, called a "jam." The other riders on the track reacted

(continued on page 13)

Top left: 1927, Madison Square Garden. In the sports world, Madison Square Garden represented both a destination in New York City's Manhattan and a state of mind. Audiences were entertained by Buffalo Bill's Wild West Show, three-ring circuses, automobile shows, Boy Scout jamborees, political conventions, bathing beauty contests, and international Six-Day bicycle races that paid the cycling world's richest purses.

Top right: Spring 1929, Madison Square Garden. The 46th annual Six-Day race in the Garden.

Bottom left: 1933 Madison Square Garden. Despite the Great Depression, which threw more than a quarter of the workforce out on the streets, the 55th International Six-Day Bike Race, November 26 to December 2, 1933, drew a big attendance.

Bottom right: Boston Arena, Six-Day Team Race, November 5 to 10, 1917.

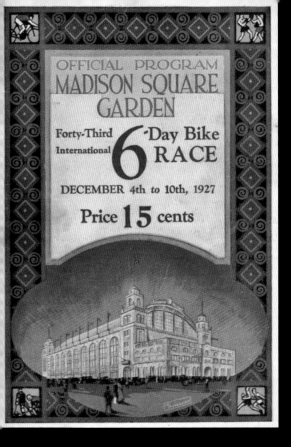

OFFICIAL PROGRAM
MADISON SQUARE
GARDEN

Forty-Third
International 6-Day Bike
RACE

DECEMBER 4th to 10th, 1927

Price 15 cents

15¢ Official Program 15¢
6-DAY BIKE RACE

46TH
International
6-Day
Bike Race
Mar. 3rd
to 9th-29

MADISON SQUARE GARDEN

6-DAY BIKE RACE

OFFICIAL
15¢
PROGRAM

55th
INTERNATIONAL
6-DAY BIKE RACE
Nov. 26 to Dec. 2, 1933

MADISON SQUARE GARDEN

PRICE TEN CENTS

OFFICIAL PROGRAMME

Twelfth Annual International
SIX DAY TEAM RACE

CYCLE RACING ASSOCIATION, INC.
A. A. McLEAN and NAT BUTLER, Managers

November 5-10, 1917
BOSTON ARENA

Music Furnished by McNamara

THE BAILEY PRESS ◆ BOSTON, MASS.

OFFICIAL PROGRAM
SIX-DAY
DANCING RACE

PRICE
25c
Pay No
More

COLISEUM — CHICAGO
July 15-21-1928

DANCING RACE

Chicago Coliseum. In 1928, Six-Day bicycle races packed more drama than marathon dancers.

(continued from page 10)

immediately, because it took only ten seconds to whiz around.

Meanwhile, team trainers scrambled to find partners and rushed them onto the oval to mount the chase. Each team had a rider tearing around the track, pedaling for all he was worth, while the other partner, riding slowly high up on the track, awaited the right time to dash down the steep banking at top speed and take over, as the spectators who packed the building jumped to their feet and shouted encouragement. The building, transformed into a riot of noise, vibrated with excitement.

Stars such as Alf Goullet, Bobby Walthour Sr., his son Bobby Jr., and Reggie McNamara rated as some of America's best-paid athletes. Road races, a European phenomenon, were free to the public willing to wait along the route for hours to catch a glimpse of passing riders. To stimulate circulation, newspapers sponsored road races, including the Tour de France.

Track events were a different commercial enterprise. They drew people who bought tickets to enter the building and watch cycling's aristocrats display their prodigious talents.

Cyclists whirled in a pack so close together that they looked like a glowing comet, matching the brilliance of the Roaring Twenties. Sixes were a mix of athletic competition, spectacle, and—above all—an American sports tradition.

SAINT LOUIS FIRST INTERNATIONAL
SIX-DAY BIKE RACE

PRICE
10c
OFFICIAL PROGRAM
PRICE
10c

"STEAL" A LAP, SET OFF A "JAM"

1933

Chicago Stadium. A steel and concrete structure constructed in 1928 in Chicago's West End, the Chicago Stadium filled a city block and featured classic Greek architectural design. Around the top of the building, 89 feet above the ground, were panels depicting athletes, carved in the ancient Greek style of Olympic athletes, including a track cyclist. The Chicago stadium was renowned for its huge pipe organ. When the organist played "Pennies from Heaven," spectators tossed pennies that rained down on the track.

Left: 1930, Montreal Forum,

Third International Six-Day

race, Oct. 12 to 18.

Right: 1935, Los Angeles,

at the Olympic Auditorium,

March 8 to 14, sponsored

by the Screen Actors Guild.

OFFICIAL PROGRAM

MIL·WAUKEE'S
FIFTH INTERNATIONAL

6 DAY
BIKE
RACE..

Auditorium

January 16 to 22, 1936

10¢

OFFICIAL ▪▪ PROGRAM

6 DAY BIKE RACE

Seventh International Race

10c FEBRUARY 23 to MARCH 1, 1936   MILWAUKEE AUDITORIUM

INTERNATIONAL AMPHITHEATRE
42nd and Halsted Sts. — Chicago, Illinois

COMPLIMENTARY

MCH. 21 1957

THURSDAY EVENING
SIX DAY BIKE RACE

COMPLIMENTARY
RESERVED SECTION

ADMIT ONE — GOOD THIS DATE ONLY

GOOD ONLY THURSDAY EVG. MCH. 21 1957

COMPLIMENTARY
ADMIT ONE
RESERVED SECTION
International Amphitheatre
SIX DAY BIKE RACE

Six Day Bicycle Race

CHICAGO COLISEUM ● JAN. 25 to 31

Trackside Pass — Admit 2

THURSDAY, JANUARY 29

THIS PASS MUST BE EXCHANGED at the COLISEUM or HUB BOX OFFICE, Jackson and State, and upon payment of Sixty Cents (Per Person) will admit Two on Sunday, Monday, Tuesday or Wednesday, January 25, 26, 27, 28, to a Reserved Trackside Seat (Box Office Value $1.10). Hub Box Office opens Jan. 19th; Coliseum, Jan. 24th.
32

Six Day Bicycle Race

CHICAGO COLISEUM ● JAN. 25 to 31

SPECIAL Pass — Admit 2

SUN. JAN. 25   TUES. JAN. 27
MON. JAN. 26   WED. JAN. 28

THIS PASS MUST BE EXCHANGED at the COLISEUM BOX OFFICE, and upon payment of Forty Cents (Per Person) will admit Two on Sunday, Monday, Tuesday or Wednesday, Jan. 25, 26, 27, 28, to a Balcony Seat. Coliseum Box Office opens Jan. 24th.
32

Facing page: 1936, Milwaukee. For ten years starting in 1932, Milwaukee hosted international Six-Day races. This cover features William "Torchy" Peden of Canada, who won three Six-Day races in Milwaukee.

This page: Tickets, please. Ticket sales generated the revenue that made Six-Day races lucrative.

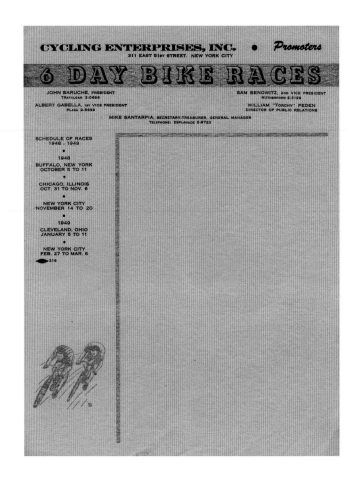

Left: Purchasing a
program sometimes gave
spectators a tip on where
to buy diamonds.

Right: Colorful stationery
for colorful races.

Bottom: Stationery for The
Garden's Six-Day race
doubled as advertising.

Facing page: Autographed
program cover of a Six-Day
race in Chicago's Stadium.

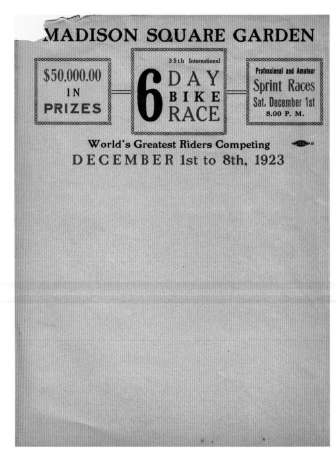

THE EA

THE EARLY DAYS

1875–1899

It all started in the 1870s with the introduction of high-wheel bicycles. Today they may look awkward. Yet high-wheelers represented break-through technology. They featured new lightweight hollow steel tubes, hard-rubber tires on tangent-spoke wheels to soften the ride, and ball bearings in the steering column, pedals, and wheels, which made them fast, nimble, and efficient.

RLY DAYS

They also made a big leap over earlier primitive two-wheel velocipedes from France, with heavy cast-iron frames and wheels that rendered them impractical when navigating hills. In the late 19th century, high-wheelers represented a transportation revolution. For the first time in history, people were liberated from having to hitch or saddle a horse to travel beyond walking distance.

Sixes started as an exhibition on a flat track in a square room in 1875 in Birmingham, England. A handful of riders pedaled twelve hours a day Monday through Saturday—stopping only for Sunday.

In 1879, Sixes crossed the Atlantic. Jack Haverly, a vaudevillian who originated the concept of a theater chain in the United States, brought over a team of high-wheeler riders—Charles Terront of Paris and Englishmen Billie Cann and Harry Etherington. They put on exhibitions lasting up to six hours a day in roller-skating rinks in Chicago and Boston. Thousands of people eagerly paid to watch these pioneer professional athletes ride on two wheels.

English expatriate and leading trainer Tom Eck organized the first Six-Day race, complete with night-and-day racing, in the United States. That was in the summer of 1887, around the Washington Roller Skating rink in Minneapolis. Eck had built the track of eight laps to the mile with banked turns for riders to take the sharp turns at full speed. Albert Schock of Germany rode 1,409 miles to win against two others.

In October 1891, Eck took his go-as-you-please Six-Day contest to the newly christened Madison Square Garden. Named after U.S. President James Madison, its entrance off Madison Avenue was graced by Roman colonnades of lavender marble. Designed by Stanford White, Madison Square Garden stood as an imposing Moorish castle of yellow brick and Pompeian terra-cotta. Its massive auditorium of pale red walls soaring up to eighty feet had plenty of room to accommodate a board bicycle track of ten laps to the mile, surrounded by seating for 8,000.

"Plugger Bill" Martin of Lowell, Massachusetts, left thirteen opponents behind as he pedaled 1,446 miles in 142 hours—from 12:01 a.m. Monday through 10 p.m. Saturday. For his victory in the Garden's first Six-Day, he was awarded $2,000—at a time when the average worker's wages amounted to only $500 annually.

Soon the modern safety bicycle with the diamond frame, both wheels the same size, and pneumatic tires supplanted the high-wheeler. The technology shift resembled the one that occurred when mainframe computer processors were overtaken by PCs. The diamond frame and pneumatic tires created mass appeal across social-economic

(continued on page 28)

Top left: Pioneer professionals Etherington with Billy Cann of Yorkshire joined Charles Terront of Paris in their cycling kit at the Chicago Six-Day race in 1879, the first Six in the United States. The long line of international professional cyclists starts with these men.

Top center: Harry Etherington (1855–1938). Organizer of the first trans-Atlantic Six-Day cycling exhibition, Etherington posed in Chicago with his English-made high-wheeler. A native of Kent County, in southern England, he had apprenticed in the stationery and bookbinding trade. He organized the first Six-Day race at the Agricultural Hall in London's Islington borough in 1878 before taking his Sixes to Chicago, making him a major cycling manager.

Top right: Charlie Miller (1875–1951). Miller of Chicago

married his fiancée Genevieve on his way to winning the December 1898 go-as-you-please individual Six-Day in Madison Square Garden. Fifty years later, on December 18, 1948, the couple celebrated their golden anniversary with son Charlie Jr. at the Edgewater Beach Hotel in Chicago.

Below: New Haven Flyer. 1884 was the year Mark Twain published *The Adventures of Huckleberry Finn*, Lewis Waterman of New York City developed the fountain pen, and Louis B. Hamilton of Yale (Class of 1886) won a national collegiate championship title on his high-

wheel bicycle. Hamilton was the first American collegiate cycling champion to gain wide attention. He wore Yale's Y on his jersey front—easy to spot with his upright position. The next year, he successfully defended his national title, making him a big star on campus.

Attitudes with pre-1890 bicycles. With their sultry looks and one wearing his cap sideways, these young flyers could pose for a contemporary fashion magazine. They're proud of their wheels—both high-wheelers and the new safety bicycle with chain drive same-size wheels. Note the thin hard-rubber tires: Though invented several years before, pneumatic tires were not yet available in the U.S. Once pneumatics arrived, safety bicycles soon displaced high-wheelers.

(continued from page 24)

Left: "The Good Old Days" watching the Sixes gave everybody something to talk about.

Right: Cartoon, "If you can't find your wife." Newspapers offered race coverage and domestic advice to attendees.

strata by the mid-1890s. Women had recently started wearing their skirts several inches above the ankle, which enabled them to take up cycling, and they did in unprecedented numbers. Modern bicycles also allowed building tracks with steeper banking on the turns to help riders increase speed—and distance.

Charles Miller of Chicago emerged as the undisputed king of one-man Sixes. In the Garden's 1898 Six-Day, twenty-nine pros started. Most dropped out, but Miller endured to ride 2,105 miles and win. He even took a half-hour break to marry his fiancée.

However, New York legislators were inundated with complaints from spectators. They watched exhausted cyclists fall asleep on their machines, then topple over without waking up. This resulted in a health ordinance banning anyone from competing for more than twelve hours a day.

Billy Brady, the impresario of Madison Square Garden, expressed outrage at the new law. He said: "I've never been able to understand why Theodore Roosevelt [then governor of New York] ever signed that bill, since he was both intelligent and a lover of sport. But there it was."

Brady—producer of more than 250 Broadway plays and manager of world heavy-weight boxing champions James J. "Gentleman Jim" Corbett and James J. "Boilermaker" Jeffries—and credited with helping actors such as Douglas Fairbanks Sr., Humphrey Bogart, and Helen Hayes achieve career breakthroughs, found a way around the intervention. He figured that if two riders each rode twelve hours a day, then Six-Day racing could continue with two-rider teams. The fresh rider would relieve his partner by pulling alongside. Thus the two-rider teams became known as Madisons.

Major Taylor — American Champion, 1900

Marshall "Major" Taylor (1878–1932). Widely acknowledged as the first African-American to cross the color barrier in professional sports, Taylor (left), won the 1899 professional sprint title at the 1899 Montreal World Championships. He made his professional debut at eighteen, racing the 1896 Madison Square Garden Six-Day when it was still a solo event. He covered 1,732 miles, the distance from New York to Houston, for a respectable eighth place. (Photo below) Taylor, in the middle, lines up in August 1901 on the Newark Velodrome between Iver Lawson, left, and Willie Fenn Sr.

⟨⟨ MAJOR TAYLOR ⟩⟩
1878–1932

Top: William A. Brady (1863–1950). One of the greatest innovators in entertainment, Brady helped Major Taylor obtain a League of American Wheelmen license to compete professionally in segregated America. As impresario of Madison Square Garden in 1899, Brady created the two-man team in Six-Day bicycle racing. The Wall Street stock market crash of 1929 wiped out his fortune. But he recouped when he produced Elmer Rice's play *Street Scene*, which won a Pulitzer Prize.

Bottom: Tom Eck (1869–1926). Tom Eck of England (middle row, center) came to the United States in the early 1880s with his compatriot Jack Prince to race high-wheelers. Eck rode for the Gormully & Jeffery Manufacturing Company in Chicago, the maker of Rambler bicycles, a major name in the 1890s. Eck is credited with

VETERAN BICYCLE TRAINERS.

W. B. YOUNG. W. J. HILANDS. W. F. CORCORAN. ASA WINDLE. FRANK LYMAN. E. H. TELLAM. E. W. MOULTON. T. W. ECK. D. J. SHAFER. A. E. WEBB.

building the first banked track, in 1886 in a building in Springfield, Illinois. Eck went on to train many of the leading riders of the 1890s, including John S. Johnson of Minneapolis.

Top: John "Jack" Shillington Prince (1859-1929). Born in Coventry, England, Prince competed on high-wheelers in England, Australia, and the United States. He perfected construction of board cycling tracks and enjoyed a franchise building them in the 1890s and early 1900s in cities from Omaha, Nebraska, to Havana, Cuba. Afterward, he multiplied the materials he needed by a factor of ten to make two-mile board car-racing tracks from 1915 to the early 1920s.

Right: NASCAR racing 1906-style. Racing down the back-straight of Madison Square Garden's 1906 Six-Day race.

WALTHI

BOBBY WALTHOUR, SR.

Bobby Walthour Sr. (1878–1949) lived in Atlanta, although he came from Walthourville, near Savannah. A bicycle messenger in the 1890s, he loved to ride fast—earning a reputation as a "scorcher." He won races up and down the Eastern seaboard.

OUR, SR.

With his speed, blond hair, and blue eyes, Walthour established himself as the first major sports hero from the South. Ty Cobb, eight years younger than Walthour, earned $5,000 a year playing for the Detroit Tigers, while Walthour annually pocketed more than $20,000 from bicycle racing and product endorsements.

Each winter, Walthour competed in Six-Day races. Paired with Benny Munroe of Memphis in 1903, Walthour won the Garden's Six for the second time. The French team of Lucien Petit-Breton and French national champion Henri Contenet held on for sixth place. Petit-Breton returned to France and won the Tour de France twice, in 1907 and 1908.

Newspaper reporters nicknamed Walthour "The Dixie Flyer." The esteemed *Atlanta Journal* reporter Grantland Rice often wrote about Walthour early in his career. Rice nicknamed Notre Dame's football team backfield "the Four Horsemen" after a 1924 game against Army. Before he coined that memorable phrase, he wrote this account of Walthour:

> It was a dash such as thrills one to the very marrow, one that should live in the history of cycling annals, for track records were smashed to smithereens and the big crowd lifted to its feet in the wildest outburst of enthusiasm that has ever echoed and re-echoed throughout the walls of the coliseum.

Various Eastern seaboard newspaper polls in cities where Walthour competed around the turn of the 20th century indicated that he was the favorite athlete. English expatriate John Shillington Prince, a former high-wheel racer turned promoter, made a comfortable living building outdoor board tracks. In the winter of 1899–1900, Prince and Walthour barnstormed with other cyclists, starting in Atlanta and going west.

Prince had devised a formula of building tracks twenty-one feet wide from wood planks one inch by three inches. He named most of his board ovals Coliseums; others he called Stadiums. Prince also designed banking steep enough for riders to take at full speed. To accommodate customers, he arranged bleacher seating for between 3,500 and 10,000 spectators—depending on the size of the town or city. In this way, he was able to create a string of board tracks from Atlanta, Memphis, Nashville, Chattanooga, Birmingham, and Montgomery to Waco, Texas, then to Los Angeles and San Jose, California. With his flair for promotion, Prince put on races that filled the seats, gave local heroes the opportunity to try their talents against Walthour, and contributed to Walthour's growing fame.

One of the most dramatic cycling events of the 1890s was Charles Murphy's achievement of riding his bicycle faster than a mile a minute. On June 30, 1899,

(continued on page 38)

A pair of world champions. Bobby Walthour Sr. considered Swedish émigré Iver Lawson (1878–1949) a stand-up guy at the Madison Square Garden's November 1903 Six-Day race. The next year, at the World Championships outside London, on the grounds of the steel-and-glass architectural marvel named Crystal Palace, Walthour won the 100-kilometer (62.5 miles) motor-paced title behind a motorcycle driven by Iver's younger brother, Gus. Iver Lawson won the world sprint championship, dethroning defending world champion Thorvald Ellegaard of Denmark.

Top: Bobby Walthour Sr. In this photo taken in Germany, he is paced by a motorcycle.

Left: National Champion's Belt. When he wasn't racing Six-Day events, Bobby specialized in riding at speed behind motor-cycles. He won the 1903 American national motor-paced championship, defeat-ing Paris–Roubaix winner Albert Champion of Paris in the final, held conveniently for Bobby in his hometown of Atlanta. Here he wears the flag around his waist, taking his cue from boxing champi-ons and their leather belts.

Right: Heads up. Walthour faces the camera, circa 1900 with his motor-paced bike— with small front wheel and flat bars for bettter control. Note garters holding up his socks.

Left: Constant Travelers. In 1909, decades ahead of commercial aviation, crossing the Atlantic meant seven days on a steamship. Walthour took his wife Daisy, Bobby Jr., and his daughters on the S.S. George Washington out of Bremen, Germany, to return to the United States after competing overseas for most of the year.

Right: Early streamline position. Walthour was among the first generation of cyclists who came of age with safety bicycles and took advantage of a lower profile on their bicycles. Here he crouches over a Caminade bicycle, made in Paris.

(continued from page 34)

This page: Sport Kings Gum. A popular trading card featured Bobby Walthour Sr.

Facing page: Nat Butler (1872-1943). Butler (right, here with John Chapman, left) raced against Walthour in Europe and placed third in the 1909 World's motor-paced championship in Copenhagen, Denmark. Other victories overseas include the Golden Wheel of Cologne Germany and the Grand Prix of Dresden. Although he didn't care for Sixes, Butler competed in eight, with a best finish of third place in 1903 in Madison Square Garden. After he retired from racing, he constructed a new outdoor board track at Revere Beach, near Boston where in 1920 he promoted races on Wednesday and Saturday evenings until 1931. Afterward, he became a noted regional landscape painter.

Murphy, of Brooklyn, NY, rode in the slipstream of a locomotive pulling one car. On his one-speed track bike, he rode over a board surface laid between rails of the Long Island Rail Road between Farmingdale and Babylon. To beat the mile barrier, he had to prevail upon Long Island Rail Road officials because automobiles couldn't go fast enough on the prevailing dirt roads of the era. Officials in the rail car on his ambitious ride timed him doing the mile in 57 4/5 seconds. His feat fascinated the public, which heralded cyclists as the fastest men on wheels.

Soon after the turn of the 20th century, Walthour specialized in the glamorous but dangerous discipline of motor-paced bicycle racing. In 1902, around a wooden oval in Cambridge, Massachusetts, Walthour set twenty-six new national records on his way to winning a 50 kilometer (31.25 miles) event. That year and the next, he ruled as America's national motor-paced champion.

In 1904, Parisian promoters paid Walthour an appearance fee of $10,000 (worth about $200,000 in 2005) to race there. He won sixteen consecutive 100-kilometer (62.5 miles) motor-paced races, and capped the season by going to London for the World Championship, where he won the motor-paced title. At the 1905 World Championship in Antwerp, Belgium, he won his second world title. Audiences were so loyal to Walthour that when he finished third at the 1910 World Championship in Brussels, spectators—and some newspaper accounts—placed him second, ahead of Belgian Léon Vanderstrift.

1872–1943

Top left: Lucien Petit-Breton (1882–1917). The Frenchman, whose real name was Lucien-George Mazan, rode Madison Square Garden Sixes in 1903 and 1904, before winning the Tour de France in 1907 and 1908. During World War I, he gave his life for France.

Bottom: Iver Lawson (1879–1949). Born July 1, 1879 as Yver Larsson in Norrköping, Sweden, he rode for the Norrköping Bicycle Club with his elder brother John and younger brother Gus. John and Yver won enough medals from races to completely cover the chests of their jerseys. In 1895, the three brothers emigrated to the United States and changed their name to Lawson (Yver also changed his first name). They settled in Chicago, where they rode for the Swedish-American Cycling Club. As a professional,

Top middle: Walter Bardgett (1880–1953). Bardgett of Buffalo, N.Y., tucked on the far left in the rear of a 1905 sprint, waiting for the right moment to come around. He raced against Walthour and the other leading flyers. During the Boston Six-Day in early 1910, he crashed and suffered a spinal injury that forced him to retire. Bardgett put his knowledge of the sport to good use in cycling journalism. His reporting and insights earned him promotion to Bicycle Editor for the monthly *American Bicyclist & Motorcyclist*. For 36 years, Bardgett's columns chronicled the lives of American cyclists. He is the nestor of American cycling journalists.

Iver Lawson finished second to Frank Kramer in the 1903 national professional sprint championship. He shipped out to race in Europe for the 1904 season, winning Grand Prix races in Berlin and Hanover, and the World Championship in London. Try as he might over the following years, Lawson never beat Kramer for the U.S. national championship

This page: Frank Mihlon, Sr., who owned the Newark Velodrome during the 1912 World cycling championships. Seated next to Mihlon, far left, is his wife, who had a flair for picking hats.

GRANDSTAND
TICKETS
50¢ 75¢

TWO PRO

Walthour's competitor in cycling, and rival

for the same young woman's affection, was

John Chapman, who grew up on a peach

farm in College Park, in suburban Atlanta.

Chapman's girlfriend, Blanche Bailey, nick-

named Daisy, always watched him race.

Chapman at the wheel. Chapman drove American professional cycling into its best years.

Walthour attracted Daisy's attention at races in the late 1890s by beating Chapman. Gradually, Walthour won over Daisy's affections. Soon Walthour and Daisy eloped on a tandem bicycle to be married by a Justice of the Peace and went on a honeymoon cruise to France.

By then, Chapman was swept up in cycling's popularity. He rode as a member of the sport's governing body, the League of American Wheelmen (LAW). In 1900 its membership topped 100,000. LAW members included industrialist John D. Rockefeller, artist Frederic Remington, and actress Lillian Russell. America's 75 million population at the turn of the 20th century, only one-quarter of the 300 million in 2006, supported five weeklies devoted to cycling.

Nearly every major city had at least one outdoor track. Chapman joined 600 professional cyclists crisscrossing the country to compete before audiences of 10,000 and more. The Thistle Bicycle Company in Chicago, one of more than 300 U.S. bicycle manufacturers, had him under contract. Chapman spent a season racing in Australia with other American riders, including Major Taylor of Indianapolis and Hardy Downing and Floyd MacFarland, both of San Jose, California, and Swedish sprinter Iver Lawson.

A durable professional, Chapman made a good enough living to send money home to support his widowed mother Dorcas and sister Annie. In July 1901 on the Salt Palace outdoor track in Salt Lake City, he put his name in the U.S. record books with Lawson. They set the 5-mile tandem record at 9 minutes 44 seconds, that was more than 30 mph.

During this period, more than 200 bicycle manufacturers, including Thistle, merged or went out of business. The leadership of the LAW held professional racing in contempt for sullying the sport, and relinquished its sanctioning of competition to the recently organized National Cycling Association (NCA). The NCA pushed for cash prizes and competition programs on Sunday. Masses of people who had made cycling a fad in the 1890s shifted their attention to motorcycles and the new outdoor sport in vogue: golf. Attendance at the tracks declined. By 1905, nearly all the tracks had closed, although the sport consolidated in some cities on the West Coast, in upper Midwest, and along the Eastern seaboard.

Chapman quit cycling to prospect for gold in Nevada. There he met another prospector named George Lewis "Tex" Rickard, a former Texas cattle rancher and town marshal. After both failed to hit pay dirt, they went their separate ways.

Rickard stayed in Nevada. He tried boxing promotion, considered the red-light district of sports. In September 1906 he organized

(continued on page 46)

Left: Young promoter. John M. Chapman posed in 1911 when he supervised construction of the third outdoor board track in Newark, where he organized the 1912 world championships.

Bottom: Young pro. Chapman rode professionally on the Thistle Team of Chicago.

JOHNNY CHAPMAN,
Back "in the Nineties" a Leading "Pro"
Pedaler.

George Lewis "Tex" Rickard (1871–1929). His motto was to give the public what it wanted, including 6-Day bicycle races. In the 1920s, when revenue depended on people buying tickets and going through the turnstile, Rickard put on five heavyweight boxing championships that each generated $1 million gates—something that didn't happen for another half-century with closed-circuit television. He also pioneered the crossover hairstyle.

(continued from page 44)

the lightweight championship bout between Joe Gans and "Battling" Oscar Nelson in the optimistically named Goldfield. Rickard announced a purse of $30,000—more money than any heavyweights had ever fought for. The audacity of a mining camp operator offering such an unprecedented purse generated national publicity—chiefly loud laughter. But the hardboiled managers of Gans and Nelson took Rickard seriously. Instead of the usual twelve rounds, the fight lasted an epic forty-two rounds. It generated coast-to-coast notoriety. Rickard found he had the start of something big.

Chapman went to Salt Lake City and managed its outdoor track. Tired of people confusing his name with folk hero John Chapman, also known as Johnny Appleseed, he distinguished himself with an initial from his middle name, McAfee. Thus, the cycling promoter became John M. Chapman.

After a few years, he visited Newark, New Jersey, where racing thrived at an outdoor board track, or velodrome. Its grandstand, with a towering, slanted roof, and bleachers ringing the rest of the oval,

seated 12,500. Only when the Newark Velodrome tickets sold out would the overflow crowd go to a park to watch the Class A Newark Bears, a New York Yankees farm team, play baseball.

Chapman saw the opportunity for the velodromes to extend to the network of railroad lines connecting Northeast and Mid-Atlantic cities. He expanded his business by managing the Newark Velodrome. He also wasted no time securing Madison Square Garden's annual international Six in December 1908. Afterward, he sailed across the Atlantic for excursions through Paris, London, and Berlin to sign up talent for his next Garden Six-Day.

By 1910, Chapman had learned about a hot young cyclist in Sydney, Australia: Alf Goullet. The Aussie had won Sixes in Melbourne and Sydney. Chapman, who admired Australians, sent Goullet a cable with an offer of steamship passage to Vancouver, Canada, and train fare to Newark if Goullet would race for him.

Goullet, flattered by the attention and impressed with what he heard about the quality of American racing, accepted.

Top: John McAffee Chapman as a racer. As a promoter, Chapman had nothing to hide. He paid his riders in full and on time. Although cyclists respected him, none counted him amongst their friends.

Bottom: Alf Goullet (1891–1995). Goullet snapped up the opportunity to leave his farm near Sydney, Australia, to go to Newark and race bikes. Here, in 1915, at age twenty-four, he took a breather during a race program at the Newark Velodrome. His world record for 50 miles, set in August 1920 on this track in 1 hour 49 minutes 8 seconds, marked the first time an unpaced cyclist had ridden that distance in under 1:50. His time remained a U.S. record through 1976.

FLOYD MacFARLAND

At six foot four—at a time when the average height for men was five foot five—Floyd MacFarland was considered a giant. He possessed a matching out-sized personality. He started cycling to deliver copies of the San Jose Mercury, *and soon ventured into racing.*

LAND

Facing page, top left: Floyd MacFarland (1878–1915). Mac preferred suits, topped with a bowler. He managed fast company, including the stellar Australian Jackie Clark.

Top right: Eddie Root, left, and Frank Cavanaugh gave MacFarland fast competition in the early 1900s, before toe straps were added to the clips.

Bottom: Original Berlin Six-Day winners. The Berlin Six-Day race survived longer than any other Six-Day event. MacFarland and his teammate Jimmy Moran won the inaugural Berlin Six, March 15–21, 1909 by a lap—ahead of second-placed Marcel Berthet of France and John Stol of Holland and seven other teams.

He especially excelled in handicap competitions—driven by his ego to make up any advantage riders had when they had started ahead of him. By the early 1900s, he had won hundreds of sprints in assorted distances in cities around the United States, Australia, and Europe. Victories included two Madison Square Garden Sixes, and one in Boston.

Teamed with Jimmy Moran of Chelsea, Massachusetts, MacFarland won his second Madison Square Garden Six in 1908. The next year in Berlin, at its inaugural Six, MacFarland and Moran triumphed. They befriended Emperor Kaiser Wilhelm II of Germany, a passionate fan, who presented them gold cufflinks.

By 1912, Big Mac was thirty-four. He had scored four Six-Day victories in eleven starts, in addition to more than 200 other victories. He moved to Newark and retired from racing to become a promoter, challenging Chapman.

Meanwhile, Chapman took advantage of his overseas contacts to organize the 1912 world cycling championships that summer in Newark. He signed up France's two-time world champion sprinter Emile Friol and new French national champion André Perchicot to challenge resident track heroes Frank Kramer of Evansville, Indiana, and Alfred Grenda of Tasmania. Their races generated so much excitement that tickets sold out in advance.

MacFarland headed west to manage the Salt Palace Velodrome in Salt Lake City. He persuaded top professionals, including Goullet, who had seen MacFarland race in Australia, to follow. A local Mormon boy named Harry Dempsey used to hang around the Salt Palace track. He polished shoes for Goullet and Hardy Downing, who had married the daughter of Salt Lake City boxing promoter "Big" Jack Price.

Chapman's world championships packed the Newark Velodrome. Kramer, who had dominated the national professional championships since 1901 on a streak that lasted through 1916, won the world title, edging Grenda and Perchicot. MacFarland's former Six-Day partner Moran finished third in the motor-paced race, as he had at the 1911 Worlds in Rome.

Mac's crew missed the Newark World Championships. He made up for it at the end of the year by taking them on a tour of Europe. In January 1913, he organized the first Paris Six-Day in the indoor Vélodrome d'Hiver (Winter Track). There, Ernest Hemingway attempted to capture in writing the drama he witnessed, but thought his writing wasn't as good as the riders' performance.

In his memoir, *A Moveable Feast,* Hemingway described "the Vélodrome d'Hiver with the smoky light of the afternoon and the high-banked wooden track and the whirring sound the tires made on

(continued on page 55)

Top: Jackie Clark (1887–1959). Clark grew up near Melbourne and traveled the world before settling in San Francisco. One of the most versatile riders of his generation, Clark won everything from sprints to Sixes. He teamed up with Walter Rutt of Germany to win Sixes in New York and Berlin, among five Six-Day triumphs in fifteen starts.

Bottom: Alfred Grenda (1889–1989). From Georges River, Tasmania, Grenda won several Tasmanian national championships and moved to the United States, where he achieved greatness. He won eight Sixes while paired with some of the best in the sport, including Goullet, Reggie McNamara, and Swiss ace Oscar Egg. Grenda also set a world record for two-thirds of a mile.

Sartorial riders. Goullet, left, and his partner Grenda on a training ride. They won two Garden Six-Day races together. They both lived long: Grenda lived to be 100, and Goullet 103.

)) GOULLET & GRENDA ((

Left: Joe Fogler (1884–1930). Fogler grew up in Brooklyn, New York, and became a stalwart Six-Day rider. Depicted here in 1911, he achieved nine Six-Day victories in twenty-six starts on both sides of the Atlantic. Five of those wins were in Madison Square Garden. Fogler never left the Garden—after retiring, he worked as an usher.

Right: Staying sharp. Jackie Clark kept a low profile cruising on the boards. Like many of his era, Clark sprinted from the saddle, like a poker player keeping his cards to his vest, and accelerated sharply up to 160 rpm.

(continued from page 50)

the wood as the riders passed, the effort and tactics as the riders climbed and plunged, each one a part of his machine."

At MacFarland's Paris Six, 15,000 spectators crammed every seat and packed the infield to watch sixteen teams from seven countries and three continents. Among them were two Tour de France champions, Petit-Breton and Octave Lapize, and the admired Walthour. Goullet, partnered with Joe Fogler of Brooklyn, won. Lapize and French national champion Victor Dupré were second. The U.S. team of Walthour and George Wiley of Syracuse, New York, came in third. (MacFarland's Paris Six outlived them all, except Goullet, continuing through 1989.)

MacFarland's retinue continued traveling around Europe. His entourage included German star Walter Rutt, who had skipped his homeland's military draft to race in the United States. If Rutt returned to Germany, he risked arrest. MacFarland wanted to take Rutt and the others to Berlin, and according to Alf Goullet, he called

Kaiser Wilhelm on the telephone and fixed it up for Rutt to accompany him. That made Rutt eligible to participate in the 1913 World Championships in Leipzig, where he won the professional sprint title.

With his easy smile, charm, and knack for telling stories, MacFarland was a magnet for reporters. They considered him well educated. He had graduated from high school at a time when the majority of his generation worked full-time on a farm or apprenticed in a trade after the age of twelve. He dreamed up publicity for his races by giving some riders catchy nicknames and wrote humorous letters to newspaper editors about his stars. He signed the letters with oriental names that caught his fancy, a device that piqued attention among the German, Irish, Italian, and Jewish immigrants who made up America's fastest-growing population groups. He also brought out the best from his stable. His star Goullet scored Six-Day wins in Boston and Newark, and set world records.

"Whatever time Mac had scheduled for a race program to begin, the stands were full at least a half-hour before," Goullet recalled.

Finally MacFarland succeeded in wresting the Garden's Sixes from Chapman. In the December 1914 Garden Six of 142 hours, Mac paired Goullet and Grenda against hardy professionals representing five countries. Goullet and Grenda rode a new winning record of 2,759.2 miles—the distance from San Francisco to Buffalo. (This record for 142-hour Sixes still stands.)

Yet Mac also had a quick temper. In April 1915, on the Newark track, he got into an argument with a workman removing posters from the walls with a screwdriver. The argument suddenly turned into a fight, and Mac died of a head injury. That put Chapman in charge of American bicycle racing. Subsequently, he was president of the National Cycling Association, which dispensed licenses to the country's one hundred professional cyclists.

Top: Three world champions from three countries. In 1915, the outdoor board track in Newark, New Jersey, drew the sport's best talent. Walter Rutt (left) of Germany won the 1913 world professional sprint championship in Leipzig, Germany. Bob Spears (center) of Australia won the 1920 world professional sprint title in Antwerp, Belgium. Jimmy Moran of Chelsea, Massachusetts (right), won the amateur two-mile crown at the 1899 Montreal world championships. As a professional, Moran won two bronze medals in the motor-paced world championships. Rutt, Spears, and Moran together won a total of seventeen Six-Day races.

Eddie Root (1880–1956). A native of Sweden, Root excelled at sprinting and Six-Day races. His talents allowed him to travel widely. He won eight Sixes—four in Madison Square Garden between 1904 and 1910, and others in Atlanta, Atlantic City, Brussels, and Toronto. After he retired from racing, Root worked as chauffeur for celebrities, including "Diamond" Jim Brady and Al Jolson.

International race of four world-record holders. From left to right: Iver Lawson of Sweden, Australians Alf Goullet and Jackie Clark, and Frank Kramer of Evansville, Indiana on the Newark Velodrome in the summer of 1911. Note the stance of Kramer's trainer preparing to give him a hard push.

((INTERNATIONAL RACE))

Left: Frank Kramer
(1880–1958). Large-jawed
Kramer of Evansville,
Indiana, built one of the
most robust careers in
American cycling, with
more than 500 professional
victories on two continents.
Among them were two ama-
teur national champi-
onships, eighteen national
professional sprint titles,
the Grand Prix de Paris
twice, and the 1912 world
championship. He won the
1910 Boston Six with Jim
Moran. A stickler for regular
hours, Kramer rode eight
Sixes, but disliked them
because they interfered
with his sleeping pattern.

Top middle: Interior photo of the
Vélodrome d'Hiver (Winter Track) in Paris.

Bottom middle: The Vélodrome d'Hiver
was Ernest Hemingway's favorite track
when he lived in Paris.

MacFarland, elbows resting on his knees, contemplates one of his final races in 1911. Behind him, the band played popular music to keep the spectators entertained at the Newark Velodrome.

POINTS

Entertainers such as Douglas Fairbanks, Mary Pickford, John Barrymore, Enrico Caruso, and others wore fur coats to the Sixes in Madison Square Garden. The celebrities pulled out rolls of cash and peeled off $100 bills for prizes offered as premiums, called primes, French for bonuses.

Harris Horder (1900–1943). A second-generation national Australian professional sprinter, Horder left Sydney to race in the United States, and added the U.S. national professional sprint title to his laurels. He settled in Newark. Horder often clashed with Chapman over contracts to race in Six-Days.

Actress Peggy Hopkins Joyce, her diamonds flashing, had a grand time hearing the infield band play "Pretty Peggy with Eyes of Blue" and seeing the riders tear around the track to win $1,000 primes—courtesy of her current boyfriend.

The Garden's primes amounted to big money at a time when a laborer earned $20 a week.

Tobacco use was high, and smoking was allowed, even encouraged, during sports events. Overhead lights stabbed through the nicotine cloud hanging over the velodrome. "The air was dense with tobacco," recalled Goullet. "After every Six, I was coughing up mud for days."

Chapman tinkered with the Six-Day format to keep his races from turning into one-sided affairs between two or three teams. He introduced a series of two-mile sprints for the December 1916 Madison Square Garden Six-Day race. He also extended the racing for two more hours, to 144 hours—from midnight Sunday night through midnight Saturday. Every morning, afternoon, evening, and night, teams competed in ten two-mile sprint programs.

When an official fired a pistol to signal each sprint, fans cheered their lungs out. Racers fled like thieves. They raced for points awarded to the top four finishers—and cash prizes of $100 or more paid to winners. To mark the start of the final lap, officials at the trackside clanged a boxing-ring bell vigorously.

On the final day, the points for each sprint doubled. Their accumulated total, rather than miles covered, determined the winning team.

Chapman's tinkering contributed to greater spontaneity and made his Sixes more exciting tests of endurance.

The new format favored Goullet. "I was like a fire-station Dalmatian responding to the bell. When the bell rang, no matter how tired I was, I could sprint."

Faster sprinters, however, such as Goullet's compatriot Harris Horder, a second-generation racer from Sydney, didn't always make the transition to the constant demands of the Sixes. Horder took offense when Chapman refused to give him a contract to ride a Six. Horder fired a broadside at Chapman by complaining to newspaper reporters that Chapman covered the travel expenses of foreign riders but left U.S. riders on their own to pay their expenses.

"We are employers," Chapman explained to the press. "The riders are employees. We have the right to choose employees who are best in point of ability and drawing power." Chapman acknowledged that Horder excelled as a pure sprinter, especially in the final 200 yards. Horder won many summer outdoor events, yet in the Sixes his punch was blunted, and his performance only mediocre.

"It is my job to build up as strong and attractive a field as I can," Chapman added. "At this time, it seems to me the riders selected fill the bill more capably than Horder does." One newspaper depicted Chapman dressed in royal

Eddie Madden (1891–1935). Nicknamed "Bees Knees" for his skinny legs, Madden of Newark was at his best riding in Sixes. He started thirty-six Sixes between 1916 and 1927, scoring fourteen top-three finishes and four victories—one of them in New York, paired with Goullet.

World Traveler. Reggie McNamara early in his career in Newark. Later he commented, "I've been to a great many places since I took to the sport: Russia, France, Germany and England. I've met a bunch of nice people I wouldn't have known otherwise."

Top: Peggy Hopkins Joyce. She married six times, preferring a richer millionaire each time. Peggy, one of the most sensational personalities of the Jazz Age, served up thousand-dollar primes at Six-Day races.

Bottom: Douglas Fairbanks and Mary Pickford. Hollywood stars like this couple, who made more than 100 movies, pulled the press like magnets to the watch the bicycle races they attended.

robes, a crown resting on his head as he sat on a throne and gripped leashes attached to the backs of the Six-Day riders.

The only person known to wrangle a pay raise from Chapman was Florence "Flossie" Root, a gorgeous former showgirl, on behalf of her husband Eddie Root, who had paid his dues with victories in eight Sixes, including three in a row between 1904 and 1906 in the Garden. This one-time bonus took place when Eddie's career was winding down. Chapman wanted to groom young Reggie McNamara of Australia and paired him with Eddie for the December 1913 Garden Six.

Root had often complained to his wife about how tight Chapman was with money. One frosty morning over bacon and eggs, she told him she would talk with Chapman while Eddie went out on his training ride.

Flossie had been a member of the Flora Dora Sextet with Evelyn Nesbit, legendary as "The Girl in the Red Velvet Swing" for her dalliance with architect Stanford White. According to Jack and Bill Brennan, Flossie put a revolver in her handbag and visited Chapman in his downtown Newark office. She swept in, strode to where he sat at his roll-top desk, and pulled

out the handgun. It was heavy and required both her hands to hold it. Chapman was so surprised that all he could do was stare at the petite woman. She rested the barrel on his forehead and suggested that Eddie deserved a well-paid contract. Chapman, sensitive to the cold steel on his skin, heard the hammer click back, and agreed that whatever was good for Eddie Root was fine with him.

Walthour, meanwhile, was approaching forty. Thirty-one Sixes, relentless international travel, and year-round toil had worn him down. Son Bobby Jr. winced as his father, once cheered as a headliner, was now jeered as an old man. The son vowed that he, too, would become a racer and uphold his father's name. Thirteen-year-old Bobby Jr. tried to enter a championship race on the Newark Velodrome, only to have a caretaker chase him away.

"Wait until you grow up before you become a bicycle rider," the caretaker said with a laugh.

The youngster rode back to his neighborhood, rounded up his playmates, and organized a series of races around the block. Bobby Jr. won his neighborhood championship. He then set out to conquer new worlds.

Born Yver Larsson in Norrköping, south of Stockholm, Sweden, he rode for the Norrköping bicycle club with elder brother John and younger brother Gus. John and Yver won enough medals from races to cover the chests of their jerseys. In 1895 the three brothers emigrated to America. They changed their name to Lawson, while Yver also changed his first name to Iver. They settled in Chicago and joined the Swedish-American Cycling Club. As a professional, Iver Lawson finished second to Frank Kramer in the 1903 U.S. sprint championship. In Europe for the 1904 season, he won Grand Prixes in Berlin and Hanover and the world championship in London. Try as he might, Lawson never beat Kramer for the U.S. national title.

((IVER LAWSON))
1879–1949

ROARING

THE ROARING TWENTIES

"The smoky heat of the arena, the figurations of untidy hot-dog stands, flag decked, the now drowsing, now screaming spectators, the throbbing incandescence of jazz bands and gongs blended with the drone of humming tires, combine to create that strange, dreamlike, and individual overtone that is the soul of the Six-Days," noted Fortune Magazine.

TWENTIES

Fortune Magazine rated Sixes as Madison Square Garden's chief consistent profit maker. Six-Day races routinely grossed $250,000 inside a week.

They took off in the 1920s, the first decade to emphasize youth culture over older generations. In May 1920, F. Scott Fitzgerald published a short story, "Denise Bobs Her Hair," in the *Saturday Evening Post*. He wrote about a young woman who cut her hair short—referred to as "bobbed." Women who bobbed their hair were seen as rebelling against the long, upswept coiffure of their mothers' venerated "Gibson Girl" look. That story helped launch twenty-year-old Fitzgerald as one of the era's most brilliant writers. Young women like the fictional Bernice were called "Flappers." They put on makeup, smoked cigarettes in public, wore loose dresses—a departure from the Gibson Girl's floor-length skirt pinched at the waist—that exposed their legs from the knees down. "Flappers" danced with their boyfriends, called "Sheiks," to the new hot jazz played in homes on recently introduced Victrola record players and bands in nightclubs that proliferated. It was Fitzgerald who christened the 1920s "The Jazz Age."

"America was going on the greatest, gaudiest spree in history and there was going to be plenty to tell about it," Fitzgerald asserted.

The Twenties roared in with Prohibition banning the sale of alcoholic beverages. Saloons nation-wide closed. With New York City's 11,000 saloons out of business, at least officially, Six-Day racing enjoyed a surge of customers looking for entertainment. Women gained the right to vote with passage of the 19th Amendment. Babe Ruth, in his first year with the New York Yankees, hit fifty-four home runs and earned $20,000, considered a lot for baseball, but still less than what cyclists like Frank Kramer, Bobby Walthour Sr., and Alf Goullet could earn.

A youngster in Salt Lake City called Harry Dempsey had failed at cycling. Undeterred, he took up boxing and made his professional debut as "Kid Blackie" in the ring of Hardy Downing, who had retired from racing to become a boxing promoter. Dempsey had changed his name to Jack Dempsey, after the Irish middle weight world champion (reigning 1884–1891) who had fought under the name "Jack Dempsey the Nonpareil." In 1919, the new Jack Dempsey beat Jess Willard in Toledo, Ohio, for the heavy-weight championship.

Tex Rickard took over managing Dempsey. They moved to the bright lights of New York City. Rickard discovered that the Six-Day races averaged more than 100,000 paying customers. They packed the Garden in the December 1919 Six, won by Goullet and his partner. Rickard remarked, "I never seed (sic) anything like it."

(continued on page 72)

Top: Oscar Egg (1890–1961). The Swiss rider Egg set the world hour-record three times. He built his stamina by competing in twenty-eight Sixes on both sides of the Atlantic. Between 1915 and 1924, Egg won three Sixes in Chicago, two in New York's Madison Square Garden, two in Paris's Vélodrome d'Hiver, and one in Gent, Belgium. In the early 1950s, he returned to the United States with his daughter to show her the cities where he had raced and to introduce her to his American friends.

Right: Oscar Egg brought home the bacon when he won a pig in a prime.

MAURICE BROCCO
1885–1965

A crowd favorite at
the Garden Sixes,
Brocco, a native of
Fismes (Marne)
France, helped pack
the seats with fans
who yelled, "Gooooo
Brocco!" He won
three Garden Sixes,
one of them with
Alf Goullet, and the
1923 Chicago Six
with Oscar Egg.

Top left: Dave Lands (1898–1966). In the closing minutes of the March 1923 Madison Square Garden Six-Day, Lands, of Irvington, N.J., and his partner Sam Gastman led an international field that included world hour record-holder Oscar Egg. They flew around the track at breakneck speed. In the final minute, however, Alf Goullet dazzled the audience of 12,000 yelling at the top of their voices when he suddenly stole a lap. That sealed victory for Goullet and his partner Alf Grenda. It was a heart-breaking loss for Lands and Gastman. But it established them as regulars on the circuit. Six years later, Lands and another partner won the Garden Six. In sixty-six starts, Lands also won Sixes in Chicago, Boston, and Buffalo.

Middle: Sammy Gastman (1901–1995). With his curly red hair in the era before riders wore helmets, Gastman, of Newark, N.J., was easily spotted on the track. He rode in fourteen Six-Day races, with his best performance a second place with Dave Lands in the March 1923 Garden Six. Gastman specialized in racing behind motorcycles. Long after he retired, journalists recounted Gastman's performance in the 1923 Garden Six.

Right: In the days before warm-up suits, cyclists, like Floyd MacFarland, shown here, wore bathrobes.

(continued from page 68)

Rickard took over as president of the Garden and made it his "Palace of Play." He renewed his acquaintance with Chapman, whom he appointed the Garden's vice president. Rickard also doubled ticket prices, the best seats sold for up to $6.60, and boosted the Garden's purse to $50,000. And he doubled up the Garden's Sixes by adding a March edition, again won by Goullet, but with a different partner.

Taking a cue from Chapman, who offered foreign riders contracts to compete for him, Rickard brought over French war hero George Carpentier to fight Dempsey, at Boyle's Thirty Acres in Jersey City. The title fight in 1921 generated the first-ever $1 million gate in boxing. The fight established Rickard as one of his generation's greatest promoters.

Professional cycling rolled in high gear through the Jazz Age. Meanwhile, amateur racing had languished after the League of American Wheelmen abandoned competitive sports. When the Olympics resumed in 1920 after an eight-year hiatus, Chapman's presidency of the National Cycling Association and its tie with the sport's international governing body, the Union Cycliste Internationale, put him in the position of gatekeeper to select amateurs representing the United States at the Antwerp Olympics. Chapman and other NCA officials chose ten riders and a trainer and manager, but left paying all expenses to the clubs of the Olympians.

Those clubs, chiefly in the Northeast, responded by forming the Amateur Bicycle League of America in 1921, open to all amateur riders across the country. ABLA officials and Chapman clashed over governing issues until they agreed on a compromise, with the ABLA sanctioning road races and the NCA controlling track racing. Chapman reigned over professional cycling and Six-Day racing.

Below: Jack Dempsey went from a youngster polishing shoes in 1912 for Alf Goullet and other racers in Salt Lake City to world heavyweight boxing champion. He started the December 1922 Madison Square Garden Six-Day race, with Goullet, second from right, looking to add to his growing list of victories.

Top and bottom: Charlie Winter (1904–1986). Charlie took up bicycle racing on a dare. His brother-in-law said that it was a rich man's sport for people who could train all day and didn't have to work a regular job. At the age of twenty, in 1924, Winter won the Amateur Bicycle League of America (predecessor to the U.S. Cycling Federation) national championship in Buffalo. The next year he won the National Cycling Association amateur track championship. He raced professionally in a total of 104 Sixes between 1926 and 1937. While racing in Germany in the mid-1930s, he was paid in Palestinian pounds because the German marks were nearly worthless due to hyperinflation. He had to keep the Palestinian pounds until he reached Belgium, where he could exchange them for other currency.

Top: Victor Hopkins (1904–1969). One of the Cinderella stories of American cycling, Hopkins went from newspaper carrier on his bicycle in Davenport, Iowa, to setting the national five-mile record at age seventeen in 1921. He rode to the 1924 Olympic trials in Paterson, New Jersey, and won, securing a spot on the road team bound for the Paris Olympics. He was the best U.S. finisher. Returning from Paris, he received contracts to compete in Six-Day races, and participated in a half-dozen. His best performance was winning the 1926 national motor-paced championship.

Bottom: Road work. Winter training in 1928. Flat hats and wool knickerbockers helped these riders stay warm on a training spin in New York's Central Park as they prepared for a new Garden Six.

Facing page: This 1925 photo titled "Giants of the Velodrome" shows trainer Dick O'Connor, Bobby Walthour, Freddie Spencer, the unrelated Willie Spencer, and Cecil Walker.

New York Alderman Charges Six-Day Races Are Cruel

Left: $100 for 10-Foot Sprints. Cartoonist Howard Freedman (1878–1937) responded in the *Newark Evening News* to a news report. Born in Portland, Oregon, Freedman grew up in Hayward, California, where he started racing in high school. Cycling took him east to compete in solo Sixes. He also rode in three team Six-Days, winning in Philadelphia in 1902. His prize money paid for art classes. His cartoons were syndicated in hundreds of newspapers.

McN

REGGIE McNAMARA, PART I

Another Chapman import was Goullet's compatriot Reggie McNamara. A farm boy from Glenfell, New South Wales, he was five feet eleven inches tall, and possessed a strong back and an appetite for hard work.

Preceding page-spread:

Happy warrior. Reggie

(1884–1971) smiled

at the camera before

competing in the

Chicago Six-Day race.

Below: Promoting

smoke. Popular 6-day

racers like Fred Spencer

endorsed a variety of

products. Tobacco

companies saw no

irony in cyclists plug-

ging cigarettes this

way—nor did the

cyclists, it seems.

THE AMERICAN MAGAZINE *for March, 1928* 85

FRED SPENCER, Jr.
Champion Six-Day Bicycle Racer, *writes:*

"During my rest periods of the six-day bicycle races nothing is so soothing to my nerves as a Lucky Strike Cigarette, because they are cool and never irritate my throat."

The Cream of the Tobacco Crop

"As a boy, I played in my father's Tobacco barns. I learned how to cure Tobacco. The study of Tobacco has been my life's study. I buy Tobacco for LUCKY STRIKE Cigarettes and I buy the best smoking types of Tobacco—the sweetest Tobacco that is grown—The Cream of the Crop.'"

LUCKY STRIKE
"IT'S TOASTED"
CIGARETTES

"It's toasted"

No Throat Irritation—No Cough.

As an adolescent, he was hunting rabbits in the Australian bush with a brother, when a poisonous snake bit him on the finger of his left hand. He set that hand on a log and ordered his brother to chop off the finger with an axe. "I don't see anything very courageous in wanting to stay alive," he later explained.

McNamara started cycling to school from his farm home. He entered local races, plentiful enough at fairs, and graduated to regional competitions. His unflinching attitude to taking risks and aggressive riding helped him capture the 1913 Sydney Six. That led to an invitation from Chapman to migrate across the Pacific like Goullet, Clark, Horder and several other Aussies.

Soon after McNamara immigrated to Newark, he made his mark by setting five world records, over distances ranging from 1 to 25 miles. Then on the Newark Velodrome he crashed and broke a leg. At the hospital he met Elizabeth McDonough, a nurse who treated him. They married and had two daughters. She also helped keep McNamara patched together. He won Sixes in Buffalo, Kansas City, and Chicago twice by the time he added the Garden's 1918 Six to his growing list of victories.

By 1932, he had won seven Garden Sixes against the best international talent, with a half-dozen different partners. Among them was the wild-haired Italian Gaetano Belloni, winner of the Tour of Italy and Milan-San Remo, Italy's major

one-day spring road race, McNamara and Belloni also won the 1929 Chicago Six.

Some of McNamara's triumphs almost ended in disaster. In the final fifteen minutes of the Garden's December 1926 Six, he and his partner, Pietro Linari of Italy, were about to trade places on the boards in the heat of a jam when they went down in a spectacular high-speed crash. Amid a heap of bodies and bicycles, both were knocked unconscious.

The first to regain his senses was McNamara. He staggered to his bicycle. He told the doctor, "If my legs are all right, I'm going back in." He remounted his bike in time to give chase and protect their lead. Afterward, he discovered he had cracked three ribs.

"People think Six-Day racing is merely a matter of plugging from day to day until the end comes," he said. "That is not true. There is a great deal to learn about position play, about conserving one's energy without losing ground, about many small things that the ordinary spectator does not notice. A good teacher is just as important on the track as he in the classroom."

His best teacher, he said, was Swedish émigré Eddie Root, who mentored him in his first Six, the December 1913 Madison Square Garden event. McNamara and Root finished third to winners Goullet and Joe Fogler.

European promoters clamored for McNamara. He and Harry

Harry Horan (1898–1980). He left a Secaucus, N.J., pig farm to race sixty-three Sixes on both sides of the Atlantic. One of his career highlights was riding as McNamara's partner in the 1926 Berlin Six, which they won. Horan also won the 1924 Chicago Six with Bobby Walthour Jr. In 1933, competing in his 70th Six-Day, in Cleveland, he zoomed over the rail and landed in the fourth row of spectators. He suffered a triple leg fracture that kept him in the hospital for 100 days. He recovered, but walked with a limp. He went to work as a Madison Square Garden usher. In the 1970s, he looked back on half a century of Madison Square Garden and remembered that the Six-Day audiences were the noisiest, closely followed by those attending rock concerts by Elvis Presley or the Rolling Stones—ahead of wrestling fans.

Below: Always wheeling. Dapper Six-Day riders on a training ride. From left to right: Freddie Spencer, Reggie McNamara, and Otto Petri of Italy, who settled in Newark.

1902–1963

A cat nap helped him recover while his partner David Lands of Newark, N.J., spun around the Chicago track in 1926, which they won.

Gaetano Belloni
(1893–1980). Winner of
the 1920 Tour of Italy and
Milan–San Remo, Belloni
started twenty-eight Sixes
and won three—two of
them in New York's
Madison Square Garden,
with Goullet and Gerard
Debaets, and one in
Chicago with McNamara.

Horan of Secaucus, New Jersey, shipped across the Atlantic. They won the January 1926 Six-Day in Berlin. McNamara raced in cities throughout Germany, Belgium, Switzerland, England, and Italy. He teamed with Belgian Emile Aerts, of the renowned cycling family, to win the Paris Six in April 1927. Frenchman Réné de Latour worked as one of McNamara's helpers during his European expedition and observed that the Australian had such stamina that "he wouldn't have minded if they suddenly made them twelve-day races instead of six."

After competing on a Milan track, McNamara made a pilgrimage to Rome with his wife and their two daughters for an audience with Pope Pius XI in the Vatican. His Holiness asked McNamara to come back for a second visit. "The second visit was unique," McNamara recalled in an unpublished recollection. "I saw His Holiness alone, and we had quite a conversation—on the subject of bicycle riding."

CRASHES,

CRASHES, TRAINERS, AND DRUGS

Six-Day races delivered on their advertising slogan "Spills and Thrills!" A majority of the cyclists averaged two falls daily. They treated high-speed tumbles as occupational hazards. Tires blew out. Fatigued or distracted cyclists overlapped their front wheel with the rear wheel of the rider directly ahead, a chronic cause of crashes.

TRAINERS

Top: Helping hands. Pete Drobach of Plainfield, New Jersey, needed medical assistance during the 1914 Madison Square Garden Six-Day race. Note the veins on his trainer's forearm.

Bottom: Massage. During the 1911 Madison Square Garden Six-Day race, Iver Lawson received a massage down-stairs below the track. The overhead light is wrapped in paper to focus the beam.

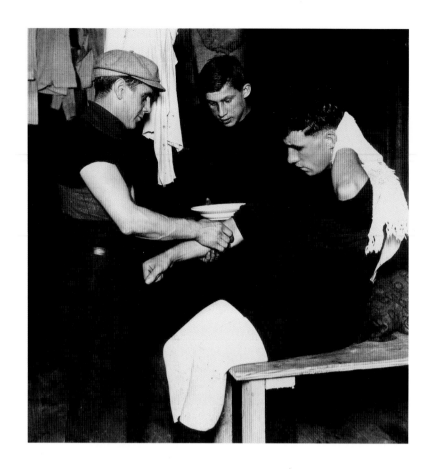

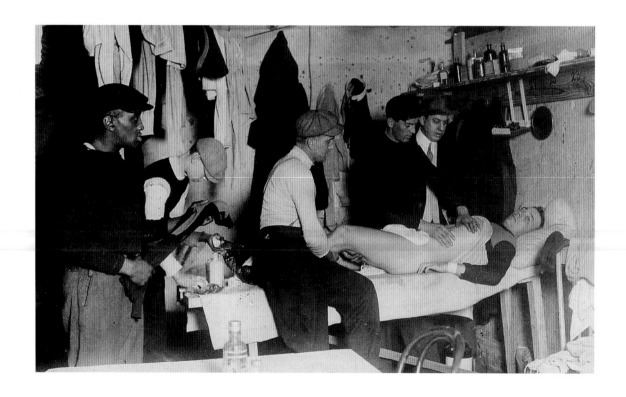

All it took was a fraction of a second, and down they went, bodies cascading across the boards.

Like bullfighters who refused to wear breastplates for protection, cyclists reasoned they were too tough to wear helmets. Some riders wore thin leather gloves cut off at the fingers. Gloves allowed a rider to grab the front tire to act as a brake after his partner took over. Six-Day riders were more likely to protect their hands than their head.

Abrasions were common, caused by falling and sliding at speed on the boards or forced into barrel rolls. Injured riders were treated by their trainers, who looked after them like cut men working in a boxer's corner.

The head trainer at Six-Day events was Fred Bullivant of Newark—great-uncle of three-time Tour de France champion Greg LeMond. Bullivant developed Donald McDougall, son of a Newark newspaper photographer, who won national amateur sprint championships in 1912 and 1913—and the 1912 amateur world sprint championship in Newark. Bullivant stayed busy year-round. He worked the Six-Day circuit for so many years, he became part of the furniture of every event.

The trainer took care of all his riders' needs. His responsibilities included devising workouts, usually early in the year before the start of the new outdoor season. On the start line, the trainer held his cyclist up. At the crack of the pistol, the trainer gave a hard push to get the rider going. He also provided extensive medical care—ranging from massage to straightening broken noses—negotiated contracts, and packed his rider's bicycles and equipment for train travel to the next event.

Jack Neville, from Millburn, not far from Newark, created a training system around the stopwatch—an innovation in the 1890s. He spotted a young rider from Evansville, Indiana, whose results were short of his potential—Frank Kramer. Neville had him draft behind a racing tandem for a lap and three-quarters around the Newark Velodrome, then had Kramer whip around at the eighth pole for the final 220 yards. Neville timed Kramer's dash to the line to determine if he went faster or slower. From there, they worked on Kramer's weaknesses. Neville trained Kramer over a series of sprint intervals while he stood, stopwatch in hand, on the infield shouting out times and encouragement. His system paid off—Kramer won the national amateur sprint championships for two years. When Kramer turned professional in 1900, he put Neville on his payroll. (Neville was also picked by Chapman to go as coach of the cycling team for the 1920 Antwerp Olympics.)

Neville boasted that he never rode a bicycle. He had such a contrary nature that he may not have learned to ride, or, if he had learned, would loudly deny it.

Top: Jake Magin (1887–1937). Not even a broken nose, suffered in a crash, stopped Magin, of Philadelphia, from going on to victory with Alf Goullet in the 1917 event.

Bottom: Jack Neville (1881–1954). Neville grew up in Millburn, a town in northern New Jersey, which had an annual 25-mile bicycle race classic for twenty years until 1908, when trolley lines were put in and interfered with riders. He trained Kramer to win the national championship and then the World's, and did the same with Australian Bob Spears, who lived in Newark and won the 1920 world professional sprint title in Antwerp. When Kramer made his final ride on the Newark Velodrome in August 1922, Neville (left) posed with Kramer and velodrome co-owner Frank Mihlon Sr.

Nicknamed "Roaring Jack" because of his behavior after a few drinks, Neville had a falling out with Kramer on a 1912 racing trip to Paris. On the return passage, Kramer banished Neville from first-class to steerage. Afterward, the two didn't speak to each other for years. Neville was hired by Goullet, and he stayed employed, working Sixes for many of the best foreign riders, though they considered him an odd character.

Like other trainers, Bullivant and Neville raided drug stores to stock their medicine bags with items such as witch hazel for rubbing muscles, bandages and plasters of all sizes, eye cups, spirits of ammonia or smelling salts, adhesive tape, iodine, sponges, ice bags, yards of cotton swabs for dabbing blood, sea salt, Vaseline, and forceps to remove splinters. They applied first aid with medicinal ointments and bandages. The final days of Sixes offered spectators a bandage brigade. Trainers did everything to keep racers going—if riders quit, they made no money and might never get another contract.

Norman Hill, of San Jose, described how Bullivant treated him when a fall had ripped skin

from his leg or elbow: "He held a big bandage with forceps and dropped it into a pot of boiling water, pulled the bandage out, steaming, and slapped it on the wound. It hurt like hell! But I never had any infection."

Mike DeFilippo, of Newark, also worked with Bullivant in the 1930s. "He was strict and caustic," DeFilippo says.

When a cyclist broke a bone—fractured collarbones make up the most frequent serious cycling injury—and had to go to the hospital, his partner would wait around to join another "orphaned warrior." Then they formed a new, reconstituted team. They received the same number of laps as the last-placed team and half of each of their respective team's points.

Meanwhile, racers with broken bones paid their own medical bills.

McNamara put it this way: "What else can you expect from a job like ours? If you can't take it, you should try your hand at something else. This is a man's affair."

Drug use was prevalent, although their use depended on individual riders. Trainers prided themselves in concocting special brews and guarded them as trade secrets. So

when a trainer like Neville handed up his small black bottle to his rider, rivals considered they had lost their competitive edge.

Some potions were cocktails of caffeine from coffee or cola nut extract—the latter making up the chief ingredient in the original formula for Coca-Cola. A popular beverage to get riders stoked up consisted of espresso, sugar, and cognac. Many Frenchmen swore by milk with cognac.

Other drinks contained the central-nervous system stimulant strychnine. Racers who felt the need for a boost added cocaine, available from local pharmacies, to drinks or ointments. Slang for cocaine concoctions was "eagle soup."

René de Latour wrote in the November 1967 issue of *Sporting Cyclist* that the punishing Six-Days required more than mineral water. "Mac had his secrets," de Latour contended. "He kept them in a small case, and if I was the keeper of the key, I never found out what they were made of. There were all kinds of pills in phials without any names on them, and I knew it was useless to ask Mac what they were."

There were no drug tests. Stimulants were part of doing business.

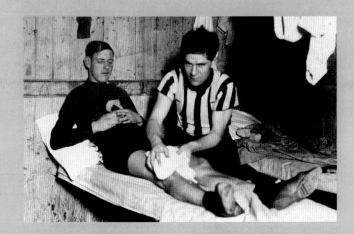

Left: Icing a knee.
It worked in 1911,
and it still does.

(FRED BULLIVANT)

1886–1942

Bullivant, of Newark, N.J., was
widely acknowledged in the Six-
Day circuit as one of the great
head trainers, commissionaire,
and father confessor. Here he is
seen holding Cecil Walker of
Melbourne, Australia, during a

Gerry Debaets gives a push to teammate Alf Letourner of France. Together they won nine Sixes during the 1930s.

Facing page: Falling down on the job. Though this is obviously a staged picture, sometimes even savvy stars like Debaets and Letourner hit the boards.

((FALLING DOWN ON THE JOB))

Far left: Spotlight on the winners. Debaets and Letourner won the March 1933 Garden Six.

Top right: When riders fell, they often had nowhere to go but into something solid while racing around the Garden's track.

Bottom right: Victor Hopkins takes a fall. He got up and continued the race.

MECH

MECHANICS

The many crashes on the Six-Day

tracks called for frequent repairs of bikes.

Those repairs were made on the spot by

mechanics, who worked feverishly to allow

the riders to get on with the show.

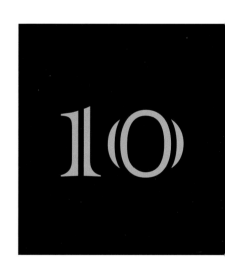

One of the master mechanics, identified in countless newspaper and magazine photos as the bald man with a buddha smile and eyeglasses sliding down his nose, was John "Pop" Brennan. In Madison Square Garden, Chicago's Coliseum, and dozens of other venues, he set up shop in an infield corner of the first turn off where people could watch.

Crashes twisted wheels into pretzels. Sometimes frames were bent from the violent impact of crashes. Brennan made all repairs. His motto was: "We fix everything but a broken heart."

In his corner off the track, he took bent frames, clamped them down on a table with a special vise equipped with a variety of jaw heads, and straightened them back to their original shape. He sometimes hired another mechanic or two to help. As soon as his sons, John Jr., (called Jackie, in homage of the Aussie sprinter Jackie Clark) and Bill, were old enough, he took them on trips to assist him—and soak up the atmosphere.

Mangled wheels received a makeover. Brennan removed the spokes, tossed away splintered wooden rims, deftly laced up new spokes through the hubs into fresh rims, and glued on a new fourteen-ounce tire. When a lull settled after a jam, Brennan stepped onto the inside of the track and signaled to the wheel's owner. With a practiced flick of his fingers, he spun the wheel, set it on the boards, and let it roll unaided back home.

Discussing his trade with reporters, Brennan said he had to work rapidly to keep up with the mechanic's job demands. Asked how many repairs he would handle during a Six-Day, Brennan replied: "It's hard to tell. Hundreds and hundreds of repairs. I'll handle bikes maybe a couple of thousand times in a race. Most of it doesn't amount to much. But then again when someone spills, there's broken wheels to be replaced, frames to be put into line. We've got to work fast."

Riders arrived at the Sixes with two or three frames and two sets of wheels. Bill Brennan, recalling the pre-race ritual of riders pulling their frames out of the wooden crates, said, "Each bike come out of the box was more beautiful than the last one. They were the best bikes from France, Italy, Belgium, Australia, Canada, around the United States—you name it."

To repair the different U.S. and European parts, Brennan stocked fifteen different lengths and weights of spokes. From his corner of the track, he did everything but braze frames.

The elder Brennan worked Sixes so long, earning respect through his work, that he was regarded as one of the Old Guard. Even hard-edged riders affectionately called him "Pop." He was born in Newark in 1888 and came of age when the Newark Velodrome was an international center. He apprenticed as a chandelier maker. The trade taught him how to bend metal tubes. After working ten-hour days—standard for this era—he went out training on his track bike. In 1909, he won a Six-Day for amateurs in Atlantic City and turned professional. Meanwhile, he started making custom handlebars for riders, then wheels and custom frames. He retired from racing in 1910, and not long afterward opened a bike shop near the Newark Velodrome. When the Six-Day season convened, he traveled the circuit.

Many Midwest races were presided over by Oscar Wastyn of Chicago. When Wastyn wasn't wrenching at the Sixes, he made frames for the Schwinn Bicycle Company, and introduced that company's famous line of Paramounts. Wastyn also operated Oscar Wastyn Cycles in Chicago, which continues as one of America's oldest bike shops.

Another mechanic at Sixes was Willie Applehans, a German expatriate who settled in Brooklyn, where he built custom frames.

Pop Brennan, Six-Day Bike Mechanic, Reinstated
By C. R. A., and Will Soon Be Back at His Old Post

John (Pop) Brennan will be boss of the mechanical department during the next six-day race. He was reinstated yesterday by the Cycle Racing Association. In the accompanying photograph Pop is seen working in his quaint little Grove street shop, assisted by his son Jackie, named after Jackie Clark, one of the bike game's "greats."

Top left: Dressed for action. Master mechanic "Pop" Brennan dressed to the nines to give Alf Goullet a hand on the start line.

Top right: Two generations of mechanics. "Pop" Brennan named his eldest son after Jackie Clark. Father and son worked with another son, Bill, in their shop near the Newark Velodrome. Pop here handles an oxyacetelene torch in the charcoal hearth, plunging the frame into the hot charcoal to heat the metal for shaping.

Bottom: John "Pop" Brennan (1888–1962). Trained as a chandelier maker, Brennan made custom handlebars and frames for many national and world champions. Here he holds a new wooden-rim wheel he has laced up and trued while talking with journalist Walter Bardgett.

OSCAR WASTYN

1910–1968

Wastyn (right) was a second-

The board ovals were made of high-grade pine or spruce. A typical track required 60,000 board feet, cut into standard dimensions of one-and-a-quarter inches thick by two inches wide, and planed on all four sides.

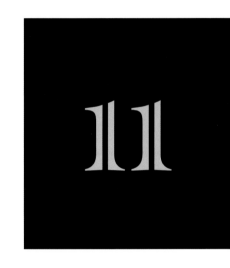

111

Bunkhouse row. Riders in a 1935 Garden Six took naps in their cabins on the track infield. During Sixes, riders always stayed on the job.

An army of carpenters erected the support structure for the towering turns, banked 45 to 54 degrees and straights of 27 degrees. The banking enabled the speeding riders, leaning over through the turns, to remain perpendicular to the track surface at all times. The boards were laid on edge, like a bowling alley and just as smooth.

Carpenters hammered a ton of eight-penny nails into the boards from underneath, so nothing poked through. Each new Six-Day track smelled of fresh-cut wood.

Construction typically started promptly after a Saturday night hockey game or boxing match. By the following evening, cyclists would roll over the carpet of boards. As the riders whirled around, the tracks made a thrumming drone. Only the audience's yelling and the infield orchestra's music overwhelmed the drone.

Preliminary amateur racing events before the Sunday night start time served to warm up the audience and tune the boards. Amateurs who fell often took the worst of the splinters.

Tracks that had too sharp a transition from the banked turns to the straights created a shoulder that made it difficult to control the front wheel and created a "dead man's curve."

The tradition of constructing board tracks started in 1886 when Tom Eck introduced a banked track in a building in Springfield, Illinois, for roller skaters and cyclists. Eck's fellow English expatriate Jack

Prince introduced futher refinements in track construction. Barely five feet tall, Prince spoke with a squeaky voice. He wore a trademark derby, bow tie on a crisp white shirt, and liberally shared bottles of bonded whiskey with reporters. In the 1890s and early 1900s, Prince traveled from Omaha to Havana, recruited local carpenters and laborers, and supervised construction of new tracks.

When motorcycles roared on the scene around 1905, Prince branched out to make more steeply banked board ovals for motorcycles. His experience, and his knowledge of different cities and towns around the country, prompted Art Pillsbury to hire him in 1915 to construct two-mile board tracks that Pillsbury billed as motordromes. Together, Pillsbury and Prince helped launch one of the most spectacular—and occasionally tragic—episodes in automobile racing. Prince multiplied the materials he needed by a factor of ten and built nearly all of the motordromes that flourished until 1925 around the United States, from Playa del Rey, California, to Altoona, Pennsylvania, to Fulford-by-the-Sea, near Miami.

At the conclusion of the Six-Day events, the wooden velodromes were dismantled and sold for firewood. In venues such as Madison Square Garden and the Chicago Stadium, the main support frames were kept and stored until the next event.

(HUMAN GUARDRAIL)

Left: Cigar track. Tracks were built to fit into buildings. Some ovals had to be built with long straights and tight turns, like this one in Buffalo.

Right: Human guardrail. Spectators lining this turn during a 1935 Garden Six-Day race enjoyed a clear view of riders jamming.

To Pete
with best regards
Walter Rutt

During the December 1921 Garden Six, Goullet was stricken with the flu. Damon Runyon, an eminent literary figure of Broadway and the raffish underworld, cov-ered Six-Day racing for The New York American. *Across the top of each page, publisher William Randolph Hearst pro-claimed, "A Paper for People Who Think."*

Runyon reported on Goullet's transformation in the frenzied 144th and final hour:

"Tier on tier the yell-tossed crates of humanity hung over the rim of the pine saucer in Madison Square Garden, their shrieks seeming to blow the riders onward like a gale, voices and emotions pitched to the cry, 'Long live the King!' Then out of the tobacco fog came ol' Al Goullet, the King that was to die. Out of the mist of defeat he came nine feet high to the strained imaginations of the other riders, and growing taller every minute. On he came, the Man o' War of the wooden loop."

Despite the flu, Goullet rose to the occasion and rallied to win. He won more Sixes in Chicago and New York. Altogether, he scored fifteen victories in twenty-nine starts. Among his victories were eight in the Garden—setting a record there—with a half-dozen different partners.

"Each Six was my last," he recounted in 1985. "They were so hard." Then he smiled and shrugged his shoulders. "But after a few nights' sleep, I was ready to go again. It's a good thing to put your bad experiences behind you."

When Goullet scored a victory with Grenda in the last minutes of the March 1923 Garden Six, Runyon told readers in *The New York American* that Goullet was, "A Man Who's Never Licked." Runyon wrote, "Chief of the never beaten, Goullet again proved that he is one of the greatest athletes that ever lived."

New Yorker Magazine writer James Thurber called Goullet "the greatest of all Six-Day bike riders."

In 1925, at age thirty-four, Goullet owned a house in Newark and had saved enough to retire. In addition to his Six-Day career, he had won more than 400 outdoor track races on three continents and set a half-dozen world records, ranging from two-thirds of a mile to fifty miles.

After the December 1925 Garden Six, Goullet hung up his wheels, married Jane Rooney, the daughter of a Newark alderman, and took his bride on a luxury cruise to Europe for their honeymoon.

Runyon proclaimed Goullet the "greatest King of the Six-Day dynasty from Charlie Miller down. Long live the King!" Prophetic words: In 1991, Goullet and his family celebrated his 100th birthday.

In 1989, Runyon, who died in 1946, and Goullet were inducted together into The New York Sports Museum & Hall of Fame with some ninety other sports legends, including Reggie McNamara, Jack Dempsey, Lou Gehrig, Mickey Mantle, Joe Namath, Bill Bradley, Eddie Arcaro, Willie Mays, Joe Louis, and Billie Jean King.

When he was asked whether there were any secrets to longevity, Goullet paused a moment, his clear blue eyes focused in thought. Finally, he let out a quiet laugh. "I don't know what works for others," he said. "But I really like steak and eggs for breakfast. Steak and eggs in the morning keep me going all day."

One Who is Comin', The Other Goin'

BOBBY WALTHOUR

THE BLOND YOUNGSTER REMAINS A HOT FAVORITE WITH THE FANS... ESPECIALLY WITH THE FLAPPERS......

C'MON BR-ROCCO!!

—THE ONLY THING MISSING..

OH WELL!!

GEORGETTI JUST STOLE A LAP!!

WHAT OF IT!!

POOR 'POP' GRENDA.. ALL HE HAS IS MEMRIES OF BETTER DAYS... THE TEAM OF GRENDA AND McBEATH ARE IN LAST PLACE..

WHAT'S A LAP OR TWO AT THE NEW GARDEN

THE ONE TIME KING OF THE SAUCER HAS THE CROWD PUZZLED........ IS HE THROUGH ???

ALF GOULLET

Below: Racing against
the second generation.
Alf Goullet, right, com-
peted against Bobby
Walthour Jr., here, just
as he had earlier
against Walthour Sr.

Alf Goullet. Goullet won more than 400 races over his professional career on three continents from 1908 to 1925. In 1916, he became a U.S. citizen and served in the U.S. Navy during World War I, stationed in Florida. He brought over his widowed mother and siblings. At Christmas time, he signed his holiday cards to friends, "Yours till the tires blow."

FEEDING

FEEDING FRENZY

Pedaling up to 150 revolutions per minute for twelve hours a day burns up more than 10,000 calories. Off the bike, cyclists worked their jaws as fast as they worked their legs when they rode. They wolfed down meals, either sitting on their bunks in cramped cabins along the velodrome infield or downstairs in the basement kitchen.

13

FRENZY

For days afterward, riders continued to have enormous appetites. Sammy Gastman recollected that he used to go with his wife to his brother-in-law's farm in New Jersey for a week to rest. "Day after day, I continued to eat a full meal every few hours, like I was still on the bike," he related with a chortle. His brother-in-law looked at Gastman and his wiry build and shook his head. "He told me I should see a doctor, get checked out. I asked him what for. My brother-in-law said the way I was eating, I had a medical problem, maybe a tape worm."

Charley Stein, the 1908 national sprint champion, who moved on to direct the commissaries on the Six-Day circuit for more than twenty years, used to say that racers ate at least seven meals a day. Reporters covering Sixes informed readers: "Seven or Eight Meals a Day, But They're on a Diet!"

"The main idea is to eat things that will digest quickly," Stein said. "They eat their steak nearly raw because it digests quicker."

For protein, each of the commissaries following the circuit routinely stocked 500 chickens, 1,000 steaks, 2,500 lamb chops, twenty hams, and sixty pounds of bacon. Vegetables were just as important.

They included three barrels of potatoes, five baskets of string beans, 18 bushels of spinach, eight cases of peas, 100 bunches of celery, two bushels of onions, 250 heads of lettuce, 50 quarts of tomatoes, 100 bunches of carrots, 50 pounds of turnips, and assorted quantities of other vegetables such as eggplant and corn.

Riders drank 1,000 quarts of milk, 80 pounds of coffee, 25 pounds of tea, and five pounds of cocoa. They also consumed 50 pounds of rice, 25 pounds of oatmeal, and 20 pounds of wheat cereals.

After a day's race, Stein said, many riders drank two quarts of milk before lying down for a nap.

For quick energy, they ate 300 dozen eggs and sandwiches made from 180 loaves of white bread, 50 loaves of rye, and 30 more made of whole wheat and black bread. That was in addition to 50 pounds of spaghetti.

Bill Brennan spent considerable time following the Sixes with his elder brother and their dad, the chief mechanic. "Whenever I was at the Sixes, I ate filet mignon every meal," he said.

Runyon, welcomed as a reporter, never missed dining in the commissary. He always left the table pronouncing the fare the best in town.

Wood-fired stove. In 1905, Madison Square Garden located its kitchen down in the basement. Not far from the dining table was a tub for bathing.

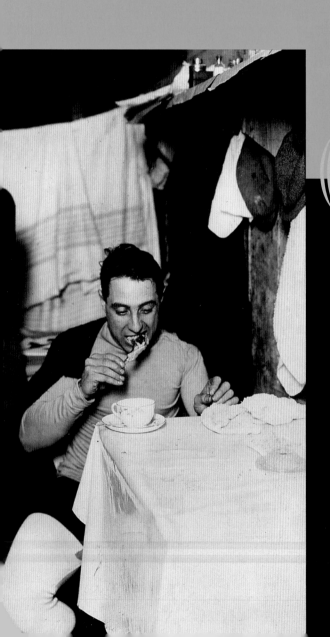

((WALTER DeMARA))

1886–1947

Dining on a chicken delicacy

during the 1911 Madison

Square Garden Six-Day race,

DeMara, of Portland, Ore.,

returned to the velodrome to

take over from his partner

Percy Lawrence of New

Jersey. They finished third.

DeMara scored a silver medal

in the tandem event at the

1912 World Championships

in Newark, N.J.

Top: 1911 Madison Square Garden kitchen.

Bottom: Welcome break. A rider at the 1917 San Francisco Six-Day race tries to recover during a food break.

Left: Company for dinner.
Australian sprinter and Six-Day ace
Jackie Clark never ate without
company—preferably women—
even during the 1911 Madison

Square Garden Six. Jackie teamed
with New Yorker Joe Fogler to win.
The cook, unidentified, made sure
he had enough to eat. Jackie's
trainer, Morrie Gordon of Australia,
had accompanied him across the
Pacific. For several years, Jackie
raced in Salt Lake City, where he
met and married Rena Bray, seated
next to Clark. She was the daughter
of restaurateur Frank Bray.

DAILY NEWS
NEW YORK'S PICTURE NEWSPAPER
Pages   New York, Thursday, March 5, 1931

X-DAY BIKERS STEAL 330 LAPS

—Story on Page 47

TAKING ON FUEL.—If you've lost your appetite and can't even eat lady fingers any more with your creamed mocking birds' wings on toast, there's only one thing to do. Become a six-day bicycle racer. You can do it in three weeks and a couple of spare Sundays by a special correspondence course. Just see how Freddie Spencer, Bobby Walthour, Charlie Winter and Lew Elder shovel it in at the Garden.—Story on page 47.

Left: Laurent Gadou (born 1912), left, of Montreal, and Frank Bartell take a well-deserved rest. Many riders recall that Bartell, who stood 6 feet 2 tall, perfected the early "hand toss" to give his shorter partner Gadou a push to take over the action. Gadou and Bartell won the 1933 Montreal Six.

Facing page, top right: Carbo-loading, 1920s style. Tommy Bello of Italy shows how it's done.

Middle right: Counter service. A photo in the *New York Daily News*, March 5, 1931, shows Freddie Spencer, Walthour Jr., Charlie Winter and Lew Elder chowing down at the Madison Square Garden.

Right: Radio days. Victor Hopkins, left, and Sammy Gastman stayed tuned in to the Garden's Six on station WMSG while they ate in the downstairs kitchen.

BOBBY

BOBBY WALTHOUR, JR.

Bobby Walthour, Jr. grew up living the nomadic life as his family followed his dad during his professional racing career. Among other places, Bobby Jr. spent four years living in Dresden, Germany and a year in Paris.

Move over, F. Scott Fitzgerald.

Bobby Walthour, Jr. had a

devilish smile.

New Jersey Jammers. Freddie

Spencer, left, of Plainfield, N.J.,

and Bobby Walthour Jr., of

Arlington, N.J., teamed up for vic-

tories in Chicago and New York

City in the mid–1920s. Frank

Kramer worked as chief referee

and enforced rules strictly.

By the time he turned thirty, he had traveled widely around the United States and made twenty-eight trips to Europe. He worshipped his dad and wanted to emulate the old man's success.

Yet in his first two years of racing on velodromes along the Eastern Seaboard, the youngster's results were lackluster. On the Newark Velodrome, he fell to the boards in a pileup that included Dore Schary, who suffered a cut to the cheek that required a trip to the hospital for stitches. Schary later would play a pivotal role in Walthour's life.

At nineteen, in 1921, Walthour Jr. won his first race, and followed up with frequent victories. He |carried off the 1921 National Cycling Association amateur championship—adding to his dad's two national motor-paced titles.

The next year, Walthour Jr. turned professional to carry on the family name—and take his revenge on the riders who had defeated the elder Walthour. Young Walthour's haystack of blond hair made him easy to spot in races in the years before riders wore helmets, and

fans liked to cheer for him as they had for his father.

Walthour Jr.'s sprint lacked punch, but his quick recovery turned into an asset in Six-Day races. In 1924 Walthour Jr., embarked on a streak of four consecutive wins in Chicago Sixes, including twice with McNamara.

Another Six-Day partner was Freddie Spencer of Plainfield, New Jersey, who had grown up watching the summer races that Chapman put on at the Newark Velodrome. Spencer, inspired by Jackie Clark's flashy riding style, sought Clark's guidance. Clark's advice: concentrate on the sprint. Clark offered a training technique. Cut a golf ball in half, set one half in plain sight on the edge of a level road, then pedal seventy-five revolutions (about 220 yards) and put down the other half; then ride up and down the road and practice sprinting between them.

Spencer followed Clark's counsel and, under the guidance of trainer Fred Bullivant, developed a sharp jump and a high top speed. After Frank Kramer had retired in

(continued on page 127)

1921 Crown. Bobby
Walthour, Jr. (1902–1980),
won the national amateur
title on a Dayton bicycle
relabelled Huffy.

((BOBBY WALTHOUR II & III))

This page: Bobby Walthour, Jr. Like his dad before him, Walthour paid cash for his homes and cars, and knew how to wear a bespoke suit

Facing page: Dad and lad. Bobby Walthour II holds son Bobby III on a beam of the Coney Island, N.Y. velodrome under construction in 1920.

Bobby Walthour (Jr.) Cartoon. "Will Ride in Garden Bike Race." When Walthour signed a contract to race, newspapers let their readers know.

(continued from page 122)

"Six-Day Riders Get Prize Money: Walthour and Spencer earn over $5,000 each for winning long grind." Enough in March 1925 for each of them to buy a three-bedroom house.

SIX-DAY RIDERS GET PRIZE MONEY

Walthour and Spencer Earn Over $5,000 Each for Winning Long Grind.

Bonuses and prize money up to $50,-000 were divided among the six-day bicycle riders at Madison Square Garden yesterday afternoon. The foreign riders will start leaving for Europe to-day.

Chapman, manager of the race, did not give out the figures of what each individual rider received, but stated that Bobby Walthour and Freddie Spenced, the kid team and winners of the grind, received $5,000 each.

During the course of the race $3,000 in prizes was put up and Walthour and pSencér won $980 of it.

The riders sailing on the steamship America to-day will be Brocco, Deruyter, Stockelynch and Egg.

On Thursday Goosens, Buysse, De Graeves and De Wolfe will sail on the Pittsburgh, while Nefatti is leaving on the Degrase.

Reggie McNamara, with his wife and two children, will leave Saturday on the steamship Acquitania for the Paris six-day race, which starts on March 30. Brocco will be his partner.

Pete Moeskops, four times bicycle champion of the world, will remain over for the summer season. Franco Georgetti, the little Italian star, who left last Saturday, will be back this summer to compete outdoors.

John M. Chapman, general manager of the Cycle Racing Association, will sail a week from Saturday for Europe. He will visit Belgium, Italy, Germany, Holland and France and line up riders for the outdoor meetings as well as the next six-day race in New York next December, in new Madison Square Garden.

1922, with more than 500 professional victories, including eighteen national pro sprint championships, Chapman looked for a rider to succeed him. He had noticed Spencer in amateur races. By early 1925, he issued twenty-year-old Spencer a professional license.

At first, Spencer admitted that he didn't feel he was ready. Yet Chapman sweetened the transition by offering him contracts of $600 (worth $3,000 in 2006) a day to ride the Garden's Six in March 1925 and, afterward, $600 each for a season-long series of matched sprints, cycling's equivalent to track and field's 100-meter dash. Two sprinters compete in the best of three matches, bringing strategy, power, and speed in a contest resembling chess on wheels. All that matters is which rider gets his front tire to the line first—whether it's a margin of a tire's thickness or several bicycle lengths—in the best of three races. Chapman signed him up to ride the Garden's Six with Bobby Walthour Jr. Chapman named them "The New Jersey Jammers."

"I hated them at first," Spencer later declared about riding Sixes. He admitted they took everything he had from start to finish. "I didn't want to ride them. If I could make $600 in two minutes riding a match race, why the hell should I ride twenty-four hours for $600?"

Motivated, Spencer pitched in with Walthour and won. He started the 1925 outdoor season more confidently, and won all his matches. He defeated some of the sharpest international talent—among them five-time world professional sprint champion Pete Moeskops from Holland. Spencer won the 1925 national professional sprint title.

In October, Walthour and Spencer also won the Chicago Six. President Calvin Coolidge invited them to the White House because he wanted to meet the two cyclists whose names competed with his in newspapers headlines.

"I never thought I would be able to shake hands with President Coolidge," Spencer told *The New York Times*.

After meeting the President, Walthour and his fiancée Margaret took a cab across the Potomac River to Alexandria, Virginia. To maintain the Walthour tradition, they eloped.

Top: Freddie Spencer (1904–1992). Between 1925 and 1929, Spencer won three national professional sprint championships. He also won four Sixes in New York's Madison Square Garden and Chicago. Spencer set six national records, ranging from one-tenth of a mile to 25 miles. His 25-mile record of 49 minutes, 28-3/5 seconds, set August 9, 1929 on the New York City Velodrome, would win races today. Scrapbooks he kept show that he finished 99 of the 102 Sixes he entered between 1925 and 1938. He bought property over his fourteen-year professional career. When he retired, he traded some of it to a contractor who built him a house in Rahway, where he and wife Vera raised their family.

Bottom: Looking relaxed. Bobby Walthour, Jr., ready to ride in the 1932 Chicago Stadium Six-Day race.

Top: Washing up. One method Bobby Walthour used to stay awake during Six-Days races.

Below: Cablegram. Western Union cables functioned as the faxes of the day. A 1932 cable to Freddie Spencer & Bobby Walthour from an admirer, wishing them success.

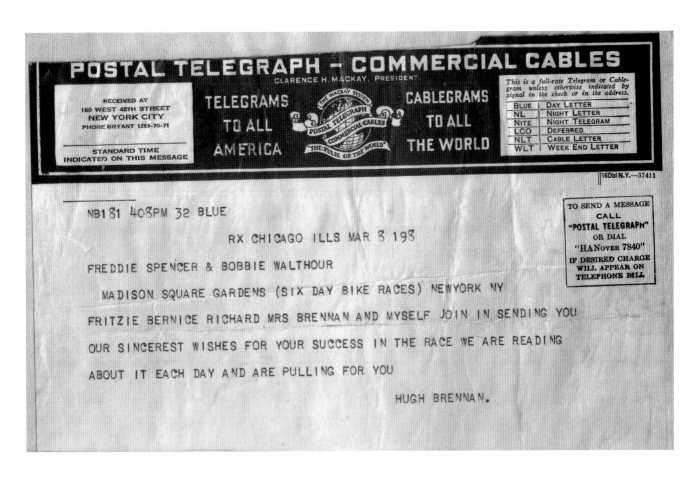

POSTAL TELEGRAPH - COMMERCIAL CABLES

CLARENCE H. MACKAY, PRESIDENT.

TELEGRAMS TO ALL AMERICA

CABLEGRAMS TO ALL THE WORLD

RECEIVED AT
160 WEST 48TH STREET
NEW YORK CITY
PHONE BRYANT 1269-70-71

STANDARD TIME INDICATED ON THIS MESSAGE

This is a full-rate Telegram or Cablegram unless otherwise indicated by signal in the check or in the address.

BLUE	DAY LETTER
NL	NIGHT LETTER
NITE	NIGHT TELEGRAM
LCO	DEFERRED
NLT	CABLE LETTER
WLT	WEEK END LETTER

16Dbl N.Y.—37411

NB181 408PM 32 BLUE

RX CHICAGO ILLS MAR 8 193

FREDDIE SPENCER & BOBBIE WALTHOUR

MADISON SQUARE GARDENS (SIX DAY BIKE RACES) NEWYORK NY

FRITZIE BERNICE RICHARD MRS BRENNAN AND MYSELF JOIN IN SENDING YOU

OUR SINCEREST WISHES FOR YOUR SUCCESS IN THE RACE WE ARE READING

ABOUT IT EACH DAY AND ARE PULLING FOR YOU

HUGH BRENNAN.

TO SEND A MESSAGE
CALL
"POSTAL TELEGRAPH"
OR DIAL
"HANover 7840"
IF DESIRED CHARGE
WILL APPEAR ON
TELEPHONE BILL

JIMMY

JIMMY WALTHOUR, JR.

Another Walthour, Jimmy Jr., son of Bobby Sr.'s identical twin brother Jimmy Sr., sped into the national limelight at age seventeen in 1927. The younger Jimmy learned the finer points of bike handling from his dad, who made a living as a "trick cyclist," popular on the vaudeville circuit.

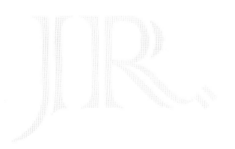

Jackie Simes II, 1936 Amateur Bicycle League of America national champion, recalled watching the elder Jimmy pedal a small bicycle, resembling today's BMX bicycles, inside a large iron wheel on a stage—starting back and forth as he built momentum until he went fast enough to ride inside the wheel to go over the top upside down.

Jimmy Sr. and his wife also performed a novelty stage act popular before the advent of television. Jimmy Sr. rode a bicycle on rollers, connected to an oversized clock with the minute hand recording distance, against a horse ridden by his wife and connected to her own clock. The clocks set on stage beside each contestant allowed spectators to compare the distances covered.

In the 1927 season, Jimmy Jr.'s first year of open competition, he won forty-five races; his closest rival had won seven. He easily captured the New York State ABLA road racing championship. The youngster achieved a rare feat by winning both the ABLA national road title in Louisville, Kentucky, and the National Cycling Association track crown, based on a series of season-long races on velodromes, chiefly in Newark.

Jimmy looked like a medal prospect for the 1928 Olympics in Amsterdam. He looked forward to participating, with Germany invited to the Olympics for the first time since 1912. When the Olympic year arrived, however, Chapman took advantage of his National Cycling Association position and declared him professional. That made young Walthour ineligible for the Olympics.

Chapman considered he was doing the youth a favor, because he saw the Olympics as only a minor diversion compared with professional cycling. He presented Jimmy a contract to ride Sixes in Chicago and Detroit, and paired his neo-pro with the experienced Franz Duelberg of Hanover, Germany. During the final hour of the Detroit Six, Jimmy's front wheel overlapped another rider's and caused him to crash. Every trainer on the track immediately ran to help. Before they could reach him, Jimmy jumped back up, remounted his bicycle, and got back in the race. That established his reputation for durability.

As Keith Kingbay, who worked for decades as the publicist for the Schwinn Bicycle Company, observed, "Jimmy was tough. He didn't pin no roses on nobody."

Jimmy and his partner Duelberg won both Sixes. The victories made Jimmy the first ever to win a Six as a neo-pro.

His turning professional also added spice to the new season's ranks. Bobby Thomas of Kenosha, Wisconsin, who turned professional after competing in the 1932 Los Angeles Olympics, recalled riding against him in dozens of 1930s Sixes. "Jimmy was a smart guy. He got by with stuff, riding through tight spaces, that other guys couldn't get away with."

Top left: Jimmy Walthour Jr. Portrait in national champion's Stars & Stripes jersey.

Top right: Al Crossley (born 1904). Crossley was a leading amateur in New England before turning professional to ride Six-Days in 1930. He competed in 87 and won ten between 1932 and 1939.

Bottom: American classics. Jimmy Walthour Jr. and Al Crossley standing with their Chicago-made Schwinn Paramounts. Together they won seven Six-Day races.

Top: Jimmy's chrome. When chrome replaced nickel plating in the mid–1920s, Jimmy Walthour Jr. rode Schwinn Paramounts with a chrome fork.

Bottom: Jimmy Walthour Jr., here at the Chicago Stadium in 1931, preferred racing to training.

Facing page: Chips off the old block. Bobby Jr. and Jimmy Jr., teamed up in 1927.

BOBBY WALTHOUR

1928

"CHIPS OF THE OLD BLOCK"

CHIPS OFF THE OLD BLOCK

Jimmy Walthour's contract to race under Chapman's management included a $10,000 bonus (worth $125,000 in 2006) if he remained single for six years, a stipulation that Walthour's parents endorsed. Chapman came up with the idea from Frank Kramer, a prolific sprinter who remained single until the age of forty-four, two years after his 1922 retirement. The announcement of Jimmy's contract, with its clause that he agreed not to marry for six years or forfeit his bonus, created a buzz among cycling fans and the press. However, some coaches disparaged Chapman's stipulation. A track and field coach pointed out

that several national champion runners, including the mile champion Joie Ray, were all married when they attained their greatest success.

Chapman's publicist Harry Mendel arranged a publicity stunt in Manhattan. A photographer took a picture of Jimmy surrounded by five showgirls pointing their fingers at him. They warned, "Don't sign."

Within six months, Jimmy, nineteen, eloped outside the city to Rye with one of the beauties, twenty-year-old Mae Delaney, who was performing on Broadway in the musical comedy, "Manhattan Mary." Jimmy forfeited his $10,000 bonus and the contract with

Chapman. When a reporter broke the news to his parents in their home on Eighth Avenue in Manhattan, his mother at first did not believe it. Then she announced she would take immediate steps to annul the marriage.

"To prove his appalling youthfulness," one published report said, "she told how she had bought him an air rifle and an electric train last Christmas, much to the 'baby's' delight."

The groom, however, had no regrets—he was in love. His elopement kept up a family tradition. And with his legendary name, he knew he would have other contract offers.

CYCLING

CYCLING CZAR

Chapman's Sixes paid well because in New York, Chicago, Boston, Kansas City, and other venues, his programs drew capacity crowds and considerable press coverage. Riders, however, detested his high-handed manner. They referred to him as the "Czar." He sternly laid down the law to prevent their behaving like some of the Chicago White Sox players who had agreed to fix the 1919 World Series, known as the "Black Sox Scandal."

CZAR

Franco Giorgetti (1902–1993).
Giorgetti, right, teamed successfully with Freddie Spencer
to win the December 1928
Madison Square Garden Six.

The "Black Sox" disgrace had shaken public confidence in major league baseball—far more so than the 2004 hullabaloo over players using performance-enhancing drugs to hit home runs. Team owners in 1920 reacted to the scandal by hiring former U.S. District Court Judge Kenesaw Mountain Landis as baseball's first commissioner. Commissioner Landis banned eight White Sox players for life. Chapman put his riders on notice that he stood ready to kick any rider from his tracks for trying to fix races.

Riders acknowledged that he paid their winnings in full and on time. He recruited Europe's best. Among them were Italian legends and Tour of Italy champions Constant Girardengo (who in turn trained the great Fausto Coppi), Gaetano Belloni, and Alfredo Binda; Swiss world-hour record holder Oscar Egg; Frenchman Alfred Letourner and Jean Cugnot (whose likeness Edward Hopper captured in a painting set in a Garden Six); England's Sydney Cozens; and Belgian road star Gerard Debaets.

Chapman signed up the top American talents, too. His fields were evenly divided with American and foreign riders. Rookies received contracts of $100 a day plus four-teen pairs of free tires. More importantly, it gave them the opportunity to measure themselves against the sport's best talents. Stars earned up to $1,000 a day. And everyone had the potential to take home more from the $50,000 prize money, plus primes beginning in 1920.

Above all, Chapman knew that spectators paid to watch the action—especially the jams. Some jams carried on for hours. The cyclists leaned through the turns at 40 mph. They veered up the banking and plunged down to build speed. Teammates traded places to keep the speed high. During jams, officials rang the bell constantly, fans yelled themselves hoarse, and the wooden oval turned into a beehive of hyperactivity that made the building shake.

Norman Hill of San Jose recalled one of Madison Square Garden's famous jams, inspired by a fan known as "The Mad Hatter" of Danbury, who put up a $1,000 prime early one morning for a one-mile sprint. "When the bell rang, the Frenchman Jean Cugnot dashed to the front of the pack and led everyone at speed up to the top rim of the track. That way, if someone tried to get ahead, he could take advantage of the banking to swoop down and overtake them. He set a furious pace. Lap after lap, I didn't think he could keep it up. And I doubt anyone else thought he could, either. But to our surprise, Cugnot keep increasing the pace. The rest of us strung out behind, wheel-to-wheel. A thousand dollars was a lot of money then, but he had to go ten laps at that pace. Finally, he had only five laps to go. The spectators filled the

Garden and yelled for him at the top of their lungs. Then we had four laps to go. Three. Two. And then the bell rang for the final lap. Nobody could come off Cugnot's wheel. He won that thousand dollars." Hill nodded his head. "It was a great performance."

Such surprises kept the fans in suspense over which team would win, even when the hours counted down to the midnight Saturday finish.

During the December 1925 Garden Six, McNamara and his Italian partner Franco Giorgetti led in points. They seemed to have a hammerlock on the race. But in the final minutes, the Belgian team of Gerard Debaets and Pierre Alfonse Goosens rallied. Debaets and Gossens, a pair of race-savvy professionals, took turns edging the competition to capture the final series of ten one-mile sprints—and racking up the points. In the final minutes, the Belgians overtook McNamara and Giorgetti and scored an upset victory.

News of the outcome flashed across the Atlantic. In 1927, when McNamara competed in Europe and visited Pope Pius XI in Rome, he also had a private meeting with Italian dictator Benito Mussolini, then a popular leader known as Il Duce (The Leader).

"Benito Mussolini proved to be just as rabid a bike fan as any boy on the bicycle path in Central Park," McNamara later recalled in an unpublished memoir. "He knew all the Italian riders by name, and he recited them in a way to indicate that he followed the races as enthusiastically as all the grandsons of the Caesars. He had me almost believing that my mother had brought me up, back on the farm in New South Wales, on a diet of macaroni."

Then Il Duce mentioned the sore spot in McNamara's career—why he and Giorgetti lost in the December 1925 Garden Six. "I was proud of the answer I gave him," McNamara said. "I am still proud of it, I guess. It sounded almost like a proverb as I said it. 'You see, Duce, the race is to the swift—sometimes.'"

Gerard Debaets (1899–1959). One of six cycling brothers from Belgium, Debaets was signed by Chapman to ride Six Day races in the U.S. He won 17 of them. After his retirement from racing, he operated a bicycle shop in Patterson, N.J.

PIERRE ALFONSE GOOSENS

BORN 1899

He did his best racing

THE OUT

WILLIE AND THE OUTLAWS
PART I

Willie Spencer of Toronto, who was not related

to Freddie Spencer, bore a grudge against

Chapman going back to 1917, when his older

brother Arthur had defeated Kramer for the

national professional sprint championship—

ending Kramer's sixteen-year grip on the

title. Kramer, thirty-six at the time, had

been one of America's best-paid athletes.

LAWS

Top: Put 'em up. Jack Dempsey, left, couldn't cut it in his youth as a bicycle racer in Salt Lake City, where he used to polish the shoes of pro racers, including Frank Kramer. Later, in the 1920s, Dempsey reigned as world heavyweight boxing champion and persuaded Kramer to try his sport.

Over the course of his career Kramer pulled in $500,000 from prize money, appearance fees, and product endorsements. He even advertised Cadillacs: "Frank Kramer, Cycle King, drives a Cadillac Victoria. Why don't you?" Seven decades later, Goullet recalled that Arthur Spencer had assumed his victory over the champion would entitle him to be paid the same as Kramer. Instead, Goullet remembered, Chapman tossed the new national professional sprint champion a cold grimace, and said nobody knew who he was, that Kramer was the star who filled seats.

"Arthur Spencer had beaten Kramer for the title over a series of fifteen designated races—the quarter-mile, half-mile, one, two, and five miles, all repeated three times over the summer," explained Goullet. "Each of the national championship races awarded points to the top four finishers. Arthur beat Kramer often that season. He accumulated the greatest number of points to take the crown. Everyone knew that one day someone would beat Kramer. Arthur Spencer finally did it. He was the new national professional sprint champion. But Chapman wouldn't even give Arthur a contract for a single race."

Arthur and his younger brother Willie, both six foot one, had broad shoulders and weighed 215 pounds

each. They stood a couple of inches taller and were more than twenty pounds heavier than Kramer. Bullivant trained Arthur to take advantage of his greater size by powering a bigger gear than Kramer. Bullivant's strategy was to have Arthur go farther with each pedal revolution than Kramer, and match Kramer's leg spin of 160 rpm.

The next season, 1918, Kramer moved up to Arthur's bigger gear. That meant spending time mastering the new gear, because at first it slowed his rate of acceleration. Nevertheless, with his pride at stake and the national championship up for grabs, Kramer charged back to outride Arthur Spencer and re-claim the professional title, his seventeenth. Kramer came back to win the title once more, in 1921. During the 1922 season, he realized—at the age of forty-two—that the Spencer brothers and other young lions had faster legs. He retired mid-season.

Willie won the 1922 national title. He and Arthur each took turns winning three national titles, but they never received treatment they felt they deserved in their contracts from Chapman. Willie raced more than a dozen Sixes, winning in San Francisco and across the Pacific in Sydney. By 1927 he traded his cycling shorts and jersey for a business suit to take over Chapman's role as promoter just as he had usurped

Kramer's crown. Willie Spencer
lured some twenty professionals,
representing one-third of the
National Cycling Association ranks,
to ride in a new circuit. His stable
of talents included Jimmy and
Bobby Walthour Jr.

Chapman retaliated by banning
them as outlaws from the NCA.
His contracts in New York's
Garden and a downtown Chicago
arena gave him prime venues.

Willie Spencer secured the
Knightsbridge Armory in New
York and the Rialto on Chicago's
north side. He promised his outlaws he would construct larger
velodromes, of nine laps to the
mile, which cyclists preferred.

His inaugural Six-Day battle
took place in January 1928 in
Chicago. He planned to follow his
Six with weekday sprint events to
draw attendance, maintain his cash
flow, and keep his horses active.

However, the track's final turn
leading into the homestretch had
a shoulder that tended to throw
riders into the air. Spectators witnessed a record number of spills
and disastrous crashes. By the final
day, the outlaws rode with so
many bandages taped to their
arms and legs that they looked
like wounded soldiers. Walthour
Jr. finished and went directly to
the hospital in an ambulance.

Dismal gate receipts ended
the outlaw effort. But the rebel-
lion still smoldered.

NEWARK EVENING NEWS, THURSDAY, SEPTEMBER 13, 1928

Prominent Riders Suspended in Outlaw Bike Movement

Top row, left to right, are: Freddie Taylor, Theo Wynsdau, Willie Hoenemann and Willie Spencer. Bottom row: Norman Hill (above), Willie Grimm (below), Dave Lands, Bobbie Walthour, Charlie Winter, George Dempsey.

"OUTLAW" STARS FIGURE TO DO WELL IN "REGULAR" GRIND

Newspaper clips reported
the banning of twenty
"Outlaws" by the National
Cycling Association.

WITH A

THE TWENTIES ENDED

"WITH A WHIMPER"

On 6 January 1929, Rickard was operated on for appendicitis, but too late: he died. Chapman had turned fifty and looked likely to take over as president of the Garden. Instead, that honor went to Colonel John Reed Kilpatrick, a Garden board member, decorated army officer, and former Yale All-American football star.

WHIMPER

George Burns and Gracie Allen. These popular entertainers fired the starting pistol of the 1933 Madison Square Garden Six. Riders from the left are Norman Hill, Charlie Winter, Werner Meithe of Germany, Reggie McNamara, unidentified, Bobby Walthour Jr., Freddie Spencer, Fred Zach (Canada), Gerard Debaets.

Star turn. Actor Pat O'Brien played the title role opposite Ronald Reagan in the 1940 movie "Knute Rockne—All American." O'Brien's Hollywood distinction and passion for the Sixes earned him the honor of firing the starter's pistol at the December 1935 Madison Square Garden Six.

On the notorious "Black Tuesday," October 29, 1929, a selling storm on the New York Stock Exchange created the most disastrous day in Wall Street's history. Banks failed across the country by the hundreds. Businesses folded by the thousands.

In his essay, "Echoes of the Jazz Age," F. Scott Fitzgerald noted: "The ten-year period that, as if reluctant to die outmoded in its bed, leaped to a spectacular death in October, 1929."

The Roaring Twenties were followed by the 1930s Great Depression. One-third of the nation's workforce was unemployed. Six-Day races represented a welcome diversion, and buildings housing the tracks becames places where people could stay out of the winter's cold.

The Amateur Bicycle League of America suffered such a drop in dues that officials dispensed with national championships in 1931 and 1932, so they could afford to hold trials to select the team for the 1932 Los Angeles Olympics. The ABLA couldn't afford to organize national championships until 1935.

For several years, as the Depression continued, Six-Day races kept a steady flow of 100,000 paying customers passing through the turnstiles at the Garden and other venues. Chapman reduced the price of tickets to an average of one dollar, scaled back the contract fees to a range of $50 to $300 (compared with $100 to $1,000 in the 1920s), and cut the prize money in half, to $25,000.

He extended the Sixes from 144 hours to 147 hours by starting the events at 9 p.m. Sunday and running them to midnight the following Saturday. During the final hour, the points for sprints jumped from six points for first to seventy-two points. Second place remained at four points.

Riders introduced a new way of relieving teammates: the one whose work was over for the moment pulled alongside his teammate at speed, reached out a hand to the other's back and pushed him up to speed.

Each of Chapman's Garden Sixes had a total budget of $75,000. It looked like this:

- cost of materials and labor to build, clean, and dismantle the velodrome: $10,000
- riders' prize money: $25,000
- national Cycling Association sanctioning percentage: $1,000
- other expenses, including promotion: $8,000
- Chapman, 25 percent profit: $6,000
- rent: $25,000

At the end of 1933, Prohibition was repealed after fourteen years by the 21st Amendment. Not only had Prohibition failed, with saloons replaced by speakeasies, but it also fostered organized crime, which supplied contraband alcohol to speakeasies. Gangsters such as Al Capone, at least until he was jailed in 1931 for tax evasion, attended Six-Day races and filled up rows of seats with their pals and molls.

(continued on page 155)

Jimmy Durante. Jimmy joked, sang, and danced his way into the hearts of everyone who heard him on the radio or saw him in the movies. He delighted in firing the starting pistol and worked the riders by cracking jokes about his big nose. Jimmy hammed it up in a gag with Gerard Debaets, who grabbed Jimmy by the nose and pulled him around the track. Riders from left are: Debaets, unidentified, Cecil Walker, Reggie McNamara, Bobby Walthour Jr., Franz Duelberg, Willie Grimm (USA), Henri LePage (Canada), Norman Hill.

Top: Rudy Vallee. Crooner Rudy Vallee firing a starting pistol at Madison Square Garden's Six. Riders from the left are Jerry Rodman, Bobby Walthour Jr., unidentified, Norm Hill, Bobby Thomas, Cecil Walker.

Bottom: Jackie Cooper. Child film actor Cooper aimed his starting pistol for the ceiling at the 1934 Chicago Six, the year he starred in *Treasure Island* with Lionel Barrymore.

(AND THEY'RE OFF!)

Facing page: Eddie Cantor. One of the most popular radio stars of the 1930s, he was known for his movies and infectious song, dance, and comedy. Cantor broke from his busy schedule long enough in Chicago to do the honors of firing the starting pistol.

This page: Alfred Letourner (1907–1975). A native of Amiens in northern France, Letourner emigrated to race in the United States in 1928. From 1931 to 1935, he rode with four partners to rack up half a dozen Madison Square Garden victories. He won fifteen other Sixes—in Chicago, Philadelphia, Montreal, Toronto, Detroit, Buffalo, and Cleveland. When he wasn't racing, he answered correspondence from his legion of fans.

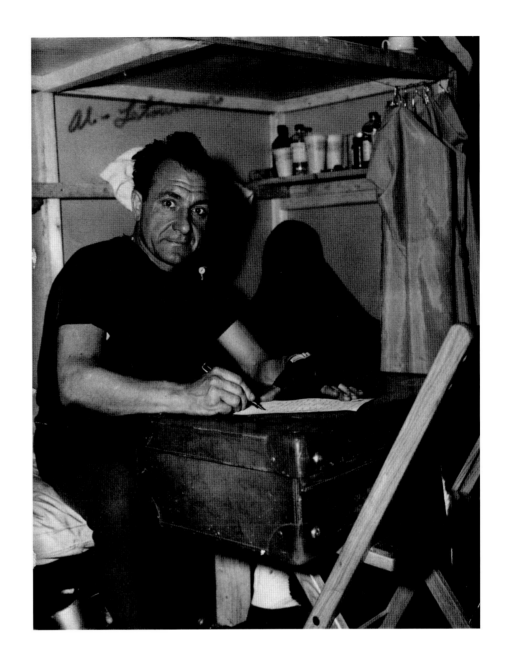

This page: Norman Hill (1904–1996). Hill started cycling to deliver copies of the *San Jose Mercury* and joined the Garden City Wheelmen in 1920. Four years later, at age eighteen, he moved east to Newark, N.J., to race professionally. He recalled that as a young professional in the East Coast races, "I didn't see any of the front for a few years." In the off-season, Hill worked for Thomas Edison, who operated a nearby laboratory. By the 1930s, Hill was a race leader.

To my friend
Bob Oliver
With best wishes
from
Norman Hill

(continued from page 149)

Tobacco companies in the 1930s hired champion athletes, including Olympic gold medalist swimmer Buster Crabbe, Bobby Walthour Jr., NCA national professional sprint champion Willie Honeman, and Alf Letourner to advertise Camel cigarettes.

"Champions in all strenuous sports prefer Camels because they are so mild and do not get their wind," read an R.J. Reynolds Tobacco Company advertisement published in Sunday newspapers nationwide. "Turn to Camels! The mild cigarette the athletes smoke is the mild cigarette for you!"

In a full-page ad that ran in newspapers across the country in 1935, Bobby Walthour Jr., is featured in twelve frames racing his bicycle in a Six-Day. In the sixth frame, he crashes and is knocked

out cold. He is carried to his trackside cabin where his head is wrapped in bandages. Soon, he regains consciousness, and his wife suggests he quit. "Certainly not! All I need is a Camel." After she gives him a smoke, he continues the race, and helps his unidentified partner to win. After completing 144 hours of competition, he poses—head bandages still intact in the winner's circle with his wife and inquires, "Now where are our Camels?"

According to Bobby Walthour III of Carmel, California, his dad never smoked. "He took the money, which wasn't much," Walthour III explained. "The Depression brought on tough times. My Dad had more than $200,000 (worth about $1.4 million in 2006 currency) in the bank. But he lost it all when the bank went under."

Racing year-round. Letourner trained at the Coney Island Velodrome in New York to stay in shape. Standing five feet three inches, Letourner's size made him a natural for drafting and competing in motor-paced racing. He added motor-pacing to his outdoor season and won U.S. national championships from 1932 to 1934.

((SOME ASSEMBLY REQUIRED))

Facing page: Some assembly required. From left: Franz Duelberg of Hamburg, Germany, Willie Grimm of Newark, Piet Van Kempen of Holland, and Tino Reboli of Nutley, Freddie Spencer and Leroy Garrison of Chicago, and Norman Hill.

This page: Emile Ignat (1908–1981). World War II interrupted Ignat's career, but his thirty-eight career Sixes in the 1930s and 1940s covered three continents, with victories in Chicago, twice, and one in Buenos Aires.

PHOTO
PICOCH

Top speed. While in Los Angeles to promote the March 1935 Los Angeles Six-Day race, Frank Bartell paced behind the fastest car in Hollywood, a souped-up Auburn owned by cowboy film star Tom Mix, to maintain a speed of 80.5 mph for one minute on Lincoln Boulevard, near the Municipal Airport. The publicity helped Bartell find work as an extra in Hollywood movies.

Top: All-Americans. Jerry Rodman, right, was twenty-two when he started the 1935 Chicago Six, with partner Norman Hill, a veteran of fifty Sixes.

Bottom, left: Alfredo Binda (1902–1986). Twice winner of the Italian road classic Milan–San Remo and five times winner of the Giro d'Italia, Binda, right, raced Sixes in Chicago and New York.

Bottom, right: Ted Harper (1917–1998). Harper, of Toronto, began working Sixes in the mid–1930s as a runner of errands for riders, and rode his first Six in 1937. He became a protégé of Reggie McNamara until World War II cut his career short. In 1993, Harper self-published *Six Days of Madness*, a labor of love with invaluable information and insights into the Sixes and the riders he knew.

1898–1985

Chapman liked Dutch national track sprint champion Piet Van Kempen of The Hague and hired him with travel expenses to ride the Garden's 1920 Six with Swiss ace Oscar Egg. It became Van Kempen's first Six-Day victory in a string of thirty-two wins through 1936. He stayed busy shipping back and forth across the Atlantic and criss-crossing America by train. Nine of his triumphs were in North America, including a second Garden Six, with Reggie McNamara, and twice in San Francisco.

Cecil Walker. (Born 1897).
Born in Sydney, Australia,
Walker took up cycling as a
child when he was thrown
from his pony and looked for
something safer. He made
deliveries on his bicycle for his
father, a grocer. Walker first
traveled to the United States
with national sprint champion
Aleck McBeath in early 1921
to race for Chapman in
Newark. Walker returned to
Australia and won the 1923
Six-Day race in Sydney, then
emigrated to Newark. He had
the distinction of achieving
three consecutive U.S. national professional sprint titles,
1930 to 1933. He competed in
twenty-seven Six-Day races.
After the 1937 season, he
returned to Melbourne and
opened a bike shop, Cecil
Walker Cycles, where he
made his own frames.

OUTLAWS

WILLIE AND THE OUTLAWS
PART II

After his failed 1928 attempt, Willie Spencer organized another group of Outlaws in 1930, this time after more planning, to make an alternative Six-Day circuit successful. Once again, he persuaded a number of professionals to ride in his Sixes. He lined up an itinerary in Montreal and Toronto, then Pittsburgh, Kansas City, St. Louis, Minneapolis, Milwaukee, and Cleveland, and Portland, Oregon.

Previous page spread:

Torchy attacks. Riding

on the upper banking,

Torchy Peden makes his

move to start a jam.

The riders he had under contract included Jimmy Walthour, recently returned from racing in Europe. Jimmy persuaded Spencer to sign up a pair of German riders from Dortmund named Gustav Kilian and Heinz Vopel. Jimmy saw they had class, and admired the way the two Germans worked together as they alternated smoothly moving on and off the track.

They joined a crew of emerging talent looking for opportunities. William Peden, of Vancouver, had turned professional after competing in the 1928 Amsterdam Olympics. Williams' younger brother Doug went to the Olympics as a basketball player. Afterward, Doug Peden raced Six-Day events because cycling paid better than basketball, still chiefly a college sport at the time.

The elder Peden preferred leading the pack around the wooden ovals. Like others of his era, he never wore a helmet. His fiery red hair blew back and prompted a newspaper reporter to write that Peden resembled a torch, and Peden was soon renowned as "Torchy."

Other new talents included Jules Audy of Montreal. Audy was riding around Montreal's Olympic Auditorium indoor track with other riders before the 1930 Six-Day, when Dutch star Piet Van Kempen observed him. Van Kempen predicted to promoter Willie Spencer that Audy had the qualities to become be a great rider if he got

the chance. Van Kempen asked Audy to work as trainer for him and his partner Joe La Porte in the Montreal's Six. The next year, Audy joined Van Kempen as partner, and they finished second. Finally, they won the 1933 Cleveland Six together.

Two others were Al Crossley of Boston, who reigned as New England's champion, and Mike DeFilippo of Newark.

DeFilippo supplemented his bicycle workouts by running up and down stairs delivering milk to customers in Newark. "I also rode my bike from Newark to Atlantic City, and sometimes from Newark to Princeton—round trips of 180 miles each," he said in a 2005 interview.

"I'm five feet six inches, a good size for drafting," he said. "When I was twelve years old, in 1924, I saw my first bicycle race behind motorcycles on the Newark Velodrome. I immediately made up my mind to become a professional racing behind the motorcycles."

DeFilippo joined the Bay View Wheelmen, a local team with a hardy racing tradition. He couldn't afford regular cycling shoes, which had a stiff leather sole and an aluminum cleat with a groove across the middle to fit over the thin pedal for a better grip. In his first year, DeFilippo competed wearing rubber-soled sneakers. Frank Kramer noticed DeFilippo's progress against better-equipped riders. "Frank Kramer worked as a

(continued on page 169)

The Pedens, Always a Six-Day Threat

Top: "Double Trouble." Together, Doug and Torchy Peden won the 1939 Madison Square Garden Six-Day race.

Bottom: Welcome to Atlantic City. Along the bottom are contestants in the 1932 Six-Day, including eventual winners William "Torchy" Peden, tallest man, in center, and Franco Giorgetti, four riders over to the right from Peden.

6-DAY
BIKE RACE

OLYMPIC
AUDITOR

MAR 8

All the
Movie Sta
will be the

KE YELLOW CARS J-9 OR 10 E

Facing page, top left: Jules Audy (born 1912). Popular with the ladies for his blond hair and good looks, and respected by riders for his all-round abilities, Audy rode 100 Sixes, winning fourteen between 1931 and 1942.

Top right: Real Babe. 1932 Los Angeles Olympics double-gold medalist Babe Didriksen, voted the greatest female athlete of the first half of the 20th Century, served as the race's official starter. She congratulated Jules Audy for winning the Montreal Six-Day.

Bottom: Deadline riders. Audy, left, and Torchy Peden together won nine Sixes. After winning the March 1934 Six in Montreal's Olympic Auditorium, they sat down to share their story.

This page: Mike DeFilippo (born 1912). DeFilippo grew up in Newark and developed as a member of the Bay View Wheelmen. In twenty-four Sixes, DeFilippo won one, in Portland, Oregon, when paired with Torchy Peden, and scored five other top-three finishes through 1937. He won the national motor-paced championship in 1941, the last year that the U.S. title was contested. On January 28, 2006, he turned ninety-four. DeFilippo is on the right.

(continued from page 164)

Bobby Thomas (born 1912).
Born and raised in Kenosha,
Wisconsin, Thomas won the
1928 junior boys' (ages 14
to 16) Amateur Bicycle
League of America national
championship on an outdoor
asphalt velodrome in his
home town.

In 1930, he won the ABLA
open national title while
younger brother George won
the junior boys' champi-
onship. Bobby earned a spot
on the U.S. cycling team for
the 1932 Los Angeles
Olympics and captained the
team. He turned professional
to ride the Six-Day in
Minneapolis with Dave Lands.
They finished second—an
auspicious start for Thomas.
Over the next eight years,
he competed in forty-nine
Sixes, including twenty
top-three finishes. He won
his final Six-Day race in
1940, in Buffalo.

(WHAT I LOVED BEST...)

referee and gave me my first pair of cycling shoes," he said.

At age fifteen, in 1927, DeFilippo won *The Newark Star-Eagle* city championship. After graduating from high school, he rose at dawn to drive a milk truck route in Newark and nearby Belleville. That earned him the nickname Milkman Mike. His day job left his evenings free to race on outdoor board ovals in Newark, New York City, Coney Island, and in suburban Boston's Revere Beach. Milkman Mike turned professional in 1931 to race Sixes under the management of Willie Spencer.

"What I loved best was motor-paced racing during the summer seasons," DeFilippo said. "I had a good rivalry with Tino Riboli in the motor-paced. After Labor Day, I did Sixes because they were part of the life of a pro cyclist. I worked with Fred Bullivant as my trainer in the Sixes."

Partnered with Torchy Peden, a rider he admired for his good sportsmanship, DeFilippo won the 1931 Portland, Oregon, Six-Day, held on the outdoor Multnomah Stadium, August 7–12. "The roads in the Northwest were uncharted—in some cases just rutted, dirt logging roads," he recalled.

While racing in Sixes in Los Angeles and Hollywood, DeFilippo noted that he and the other cyclists were treated well. "I was in the Rose Bowl Parade, met the Prime Minister of Canada, and the great director of musicals Busby Berkeley. Once we were given a tour of sound stage lots when we came upon Dick Powell. He was a big movie star. He stopped the filming and said, 'Here come the Six-Day racing boys.' He invited us over so we could get introduced."

HARRY

HARRY MENDEL

Newark newspaper reporter Harry Mendel,

who covered cycling when reporters called bicycle

racing New Jersey's national sport, had started

in 1926 as Chapman's publicity assistant.

Mendel also filled in by taking on other duties

for his boss. In the early 1930s, Chapman

handed the Chicago Six over to Mendel.

MENDEL

Top left: Cigarette break. Pop Brennan, right, and trainer Fred Bullivant, great uncle of three-time Tour de France winner Greg LeMond, take a cigarette break in Fort Wayne, Indiana.

Top right: Champagne scribes. Before Mendel became a cycling impresario, and later a boxing publicist, he worked as a sports reporter for the *Newark Ledger* in New Jersey. Here he sits between columnist Willie Ratner (left) and the paper's editor, J.P. Norton.

Bottom: Mendel's stars. From left to right: Torchy Peden, Doug Peden, Gustav Kilian, Heinz Vopel, two unidentified riders, Jimmy Walthour, and Al Crossley on a ride in Central Park, New York, in the late 1930s.

Kings of Sport. After the March 1925 Madison Square Garden Six-Day race, Tex Rickard celebrated an extravagant "Kings of Sport" banquet at the Waldorf-Astoria with the year's most popular athletes. Spencer recalled that after posing for the camera, these sports icons left for Walter Chrysler's home. They partied till dawn. Back row, from left to right: Yankees star hitter Babe Ruth; heavyweight boxing champion Gene Tunney; Olympic gold medalist swimmer Johnny Weissmuller, who would rule the jungle in movies as *Tarzan*; New York Rangers hockey star Bill Cook, who shot the team's first goal. Front row from left: Wimbledon tennis champion Bill Tilden; golf's Grand Slam winner Bobby Jones; and Six-Day stars Spencer and his partner Charlie Winter.

MENDEL'S STARS

Chapman, in his forties, married a twenty-two-year-old Georgia woman, Martha Stevens. He owned thousands of acres in Georgia's Fulton County, embracing his hometown of College Park and Atlanta, and thousands of acres south of Atlanta. Despite the Depression's hardship, he was a millionaire several times over. He and Martha liked to play pinochle with other couples and traveled between their cattle farm in College Park, Georgia—with letters five feet tall proclaiming "Velodrome Farm"—and his mansion in Summit, New Jersey. He left Mendel to battle with Willie and the outlaws.

Despite the dwindling opportunites of the Depression, new riders continued to come up in the sport. Tino Riboli, of Newark, first showed his talent at age fourteen, in 1928, when he won the Amateur Bicycle League of America junior boys' national championship in Kenosha, Wisconsin. He turned professional in 1933.

Spencer's crew made up the B-circuit, Chapman's races made up the A-circuit, which had been inherited by Mendel. Rivalry between the A-circuit stars and the B-circuit outlaws inspired Mendel to let them duke it out for top honors in the November 1935 Chicago Stadium Six-Day.

Kilian and Vopel won, four laps ahead of the A-circuit stars of Norman Hill and Jerry Rodman of Chicago. Soon the Six-Day circuit rolled into Madison Square Garden. Kilian and Vopel won again, with fellow B-circuit outlaws Jimmy Walthour and partner Crossley in second, and Peden-Audy in third.

Mendel cut a deal with Spencer, and consolidated his hold on Six-Day racing. Mendel also continued to recruit emerging talent. When Charley Bergna, of Paterson, New Jersey, won the 1937 Amateur Bicycle League of America national championship in Buffalo, Mendel signed him up to turn professional and ride the Sixes. Mendel doted upon Bergna and paired him with experienced riders, which paid off when Bergna won his first Six, in 1939 in Cleveland, with Archie Bollaert, of New York City. Although Bergna's star was rising, world events were about to trump sports.

Facing page: Occupational hazard. Charlie Bergna, right, gets first aid.

Top: Taking their places. Torchy Peden, foreground, takes a moment to concentrate before the gun goes off for the 1936 Cleveland Six Day race.

Bottom: Baseball Hall-of-Famer Joe DiMaggio traded his N.Y. Yankees pinstripe uniform for a suit to start a Madison Square Garden Six-Day.

KILIAN

GUSTAV KILIAN & HEINZ VOPEL

Many American audiences thought the German duo of Kilian and Vopel were brothers. They were the same height and weight, wore the same shoe size, and even resembled one another in their position on the bike.

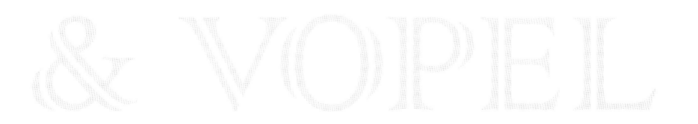

Left: Gustav Kilian. Portrait, mid–1930s. In addition to his Six-Day exploits, Kilian won the 1940 U.S. national motor-paced championship.

Right: Heinz Vopel. He was the other half of the top German team in Six-Day races.

During quiet moments in the Chicago Stadium, when the organist played a Latin beat, Kilian sat up on his bicycle and gyrated a rumba. At other times, he and Torchy Peden played a game of crisscrossing at the head of the group of riders, alternately swooping down the banking in front of one another.

Vopel had the more serious personality of the pair. He took on the role of team strategist.

In Chicago, New York, Minneapolis, Montreal, Pittsburgh, Cleveland, Milwaukee, St. Louis, Buffalo, Indianapolis, and in an excursion across the Atlantic to London, the team of Kilian and

Vopel won two dozen Sixes. When they showed up, everyone else had to compete for second.

Politics and sports made for a disaster at the Chicago Six in November 1940. Kilian and Vopel practically owned the Sixes there. When it seemed obvious that another victory was in their grasp on the final night, they donned black armbands bearing the Nazi swastika and rode around the oval wearing swastikas. Suddenly, the mood of 20,000 admiring spectators who filled the Stadium changed into hostility. Booing and catcalls so riled the German duo that they packed up and sailed home to their fatherland to join the army.

Below: Giuseppe Olmo (1911–1975). Usually remembered for his two triumphs in Milan–San Remo and for setting the world hour record in the 1930s, Olmo also raced in the United States. At the 1932 Los Angeles Olympics, he won a gold medal in the 100-kilometer team time trial. He participated in the Garden's September 1938 Six-Day race, paired with Tino Riboli for sixth place.

Top: Nazi flag. Vopel and Kilian hung a swastika flag outside their bunk in St. Louis.

REGGIE McNAMARA
PART II

McNamara's 19th, and last, Six-Day victory took place in January 1933 in Cleveland, with Norman Hill. McNamara was long familiar to fans who recognized him wearing the black jersey representing Australia. McNamara was forty-five.

Previous page: Too old to plough. In 1942 "Iron Man" Reggie McNamara worked the Chicago Six as a referee. Cecil Yates, left, and Torchy Peden won money, glory, and flowers.

Top: U.S. Bicycling Hall-of-Famer. When Reggie was inducted in May 2004, his great-granddaughter, Lori McGowan, of Lancaster, Pennsylvania, represented him. With her is author Peter J. Nye.

Bottom: Grampa Reggie. McNamara in 1947, with his granddaughter, Rosemary Zinc.

U.S. BICYCLING HALL-OF-FAMER

Réné de Latour wrote that for more than twenty years, a Six-Day race in America without McNamara was "like Hamlet without the Prince."

In each Six, McNamara, by his own reckoning, had fallen on the board tracks as many as twenty times. He suffered more broken bones than he could remember. He fractured his collarbone fourteen times, broke his nose, his jaw, and suffered two skull fractures. "I picked up enough splinters to build my own board track," he told reporters.

His trainer, Fred Bullivant, observed, "He's so tough, even adhesive tape doesn't stick to him."

Small wonder that McNamara acquired the nickname "Iron Man." That was decades before the triathlon of that name was even a consideration. His reputation as "Iron Man" was burnished in a near-fatal crash during the April 1933 Boston Garden Six.

On the third night, Bobby Walthour Jr. and his partner Ewald Wissel had jumped ahead and stolen a lap on the field of thirteen teams. All the riders were flying around the saucer lap after lap in a jam. The audience of 15,000 jumped to their feet and shouted. Walthour had made

several turns around the saucer and reached out his hand to push Wissel along on the home straight to take over the chase. However, Walthour got caught in traffic, bumped another rider, and toppled over at speed. His steel pedal dug into the boards and tore out chunks of wood.

McNamara charged up from behind the fallen Walthour and started to swing away to avoid a collision. McNamara's abrupt move caused his bicycle to tip over. He fell on his left side and slid on the boards for six feet. A splinter eight inches long and two inches wide pierced him under the bottom rib and tore away an area of flesh as large as his fist. The splinter barely missed puncturing both his spleen and his kidney. Only the prompt attention of a physician at trackside saved his life. McNamara was carried on a stretcher to his trackside bunk, where the physician spent an hour removing the splinter.

Bobby Walthour IV was a youngster when he witnessed the first-aid. "Mac told the doctor and riders and trainers who surrounded him to be careful pulling the splinter out," Walthour III recalled. "He said, 'Those are me guts you've got there.'"

While the doctor dressed the wound, McNamara lay back on his pillow smoking a cigarette. He joked with his anxious trainer Bullivant that he would continue, but the physician pulled him out of the race.

In 1934, he commented that he expected to ride until the end of his life. But he also talked from time to time about retiring. The adulation he drew from crowds and reporters kept him returning to spin more laps around the board ovals. He also liked the post-race parties. Victor Linart, the Belgian who won four motor-paced world championships and competed in Sixes against McNamara, recalled one of the parties that Mac and his compatriot Bob Spears held after a big race. The party ended in the police station. "But everything worked out O.K.—the chief of the police, too, was Irish!"

Only when he had turned fifty, in 1937, and racked up a career total of 108 Six-Days, did McNamara finally hang up his black jersey for the last time. By then he had survived more than 1,500 crashes. He had raced about 135,000 miles in Six-Days—enough to circle the globe five times.

FADE TO

FADE TO DARK

Actor Bert Lahr, remembered for his role as the Cowardly Lion in "The Wizard of Oz," and a fan of the sport, once remarked, "Racing in Six-Days is a hard way to earn an easy living."

Previous page spread: No. 13. Alf Letourner defied superstition by wearing No. 13 prominently across his back, which brought him publicity. Here he pushes his partner, Raymond Bedard, of Canada, into action. Such pushes started in the 1930s. Before then, riders relieved each other with the fresh partner riding up alongside the other. This was referred to as a "wireless pickup," after the movement by which an electric trolley passed from one overhead wire to the next.

This page: Big Picture, MSG, 1935. Despite the Depression, the Madison Square Garden Six-Day race drew standing room only crowds in 1935.

Facing page: Charlie Bergna (born 1916). On his $5 bicycle, Bergna in his hometown of Paterson, New Jersey, could outride a Ford Model T.

Since the late 1890s, warm-weather outdoor racing on board tracks such as the Newark Velodrome was followed by the indoor Sixes. Together, they operated as a yin and yang of American bicycle racing. The athletes had steady work, and reporters and photographers kept writing and illustrating articles to keep cyclists in the news. However, by 1931, the Newark Velodrome and most other outdoor ovals had closed. The only one to remain open was Coney Island Velodrome in New York.

In June 1933, a new outdoor board track opened in Nutley, New Jersey, under Mendel's management. Opening day drew 12,000 spectators. However, after a few seasons, interest waned. Money became scarce and affected more and more Six-Day races. Mendel responded to declining attendance at Nutley and on the Six-Day circuit by paying riders on commission. Poor box-office receipts in one city after another had forced him into debt.

Bobby Walthour Jr. and his wife Margaret lived with their two sons in a comfortable red-brick house in Woodridge, in northern New Jersey. After they lost their savings in the collapse of their bank, the family managed rental properties Walthour owned. They still drove a stylish Pierce Arrow that he had won in a Garden prime. In early 1937, Walthour learned of a Six-Day in Hollywood to be held in May.

"My Dad had always paid cash for homes and other properties and cars he bought," said Walthour III. "But during the Depression, he no longer had money to afford the taxes on our home and the other properties. So one night our family packed suitcases, threw them in the Pierce Arrow, and Dad drove us west to Hollywood. When we needed gas, Dad had to siphon it from parked cars after dark. We simply left our house and everything else we owned in New Jersey behind. My Dad had won lots of silver cups made by Tiffany. We never saw them again."

Walthour teamed with New Yorker Oscar Juner to win the May Hollywood Six. That generated revenue to help the family relocate to southern California. The only regular work Walthour could get was as a school-crossing guard. One day, Dore Schary, who had moved to Hollywood and worked as a screenwriter, spotted him. Schary pointed to the scar on his chin from crashing decades earlier with Walthour on the Newark Velodrome. Schary, who won an Academy Award for the script for the 1938 movie "Boys Town," helped Walthour land a job at MGM's film library.

Mendel closed the Nutley Velodrome on August 5, 1937, citing poor spectator turnout. (The track re-opened under different management for midget-car racing the next year, but closed in 1939 after three driver fatalities.)

In 1938, for the first time in nineteen years, Mendel could

Facing page, top: Town square. Bergna leading buddies on a ride in 1935 from the Paterson town square, when Paterson was still known as Silk City for its textile manufacturing.

Facing page, bottom: Charlie Bergna, right, was a neo-pro who became a protégé of Alfred Letourner, left, then a grand old man of the wooden ovals. Letourner was keeping up a tradition. He had been coached by France's national professional sprint champion Edmund Jacquelin.

This page, top: Fan card. One of the cards Bergna gave out to fans at races.

stage only one Six-Day race at Madison Square Garden. It had a strong field. Riboli partnered with Italian Giuseppe Olmo, winner of Milan–San Remo. They finished in sixth place behind Kilian and Vopel.

Freddie Spencer said that after the mid-1930s, he started stacking the prize and prime money he won and the IOUs he received. When his IOUs stacked taller than cash in 1938, he retired. "The Sixes were too hard to ride for nothing."

Mendel also felt the need for a career change. He prevailed upon his Madison Square Garden contacts and found a job handling publicity for heavyweight boxing champion Joe Louis. Meanwhile, he organized the Garden Six-Day race in May 1939. That was shortened to five days—just as well, because only half the seats were sold. Winners were Torchy and Doug Peden.

Jimmy Walthour Jr. and his wife Mae divorced. In August, 1939 he married Alyce Brent in New Bedford, Massachusetts. His

frequent Six-Day partner Crossley served as his best man.

German troops invaded Poland in 1939, then occupied Belgium, Holland, and France. Britain and France declared war on Germany; Italy declared war on Britain and France. Inspite of the war in Europe, in November 1939, Mendel held the sixty-seventh, and last, of the annual Garden Sixes. One of the few Europeans venturing across the Atlantic was the new world champion professional sprinter from Holland, twenty-three-year-old Arie Van Vliet. He partnered with Belgian Gerard Debaets for fifth place, behind winners César Moretti Jr. of Italy and Cecil Yates of Chicago.

On December 7, 1941, Japanese planes attacked the U.S. Naval base in Pearl Harbor, Hawaii. The United States declared war on Japan. With World War II enveloping the globe, a boisterous and hardy American sports era was among the early casualties.

Top: Cabin life. Bergna lying in his cabin, with spare jerseys and shorts drying on a line strung across the top of the cabin.

Bottom left: No five o'clock shadow. Bergna shaving in his bunk, with the mirror sitting on his handlebars.

Bottom right: Smell the flowers. Jerry Rodman holds a spray of flowers in 1938 after the Chicago Six and receives congratulations from Ignaz Schwinn, founder of the Schwinn Bicycle Company. Rodman won with Cecil Yates of Chicago (between Rodman and Schwinn.)

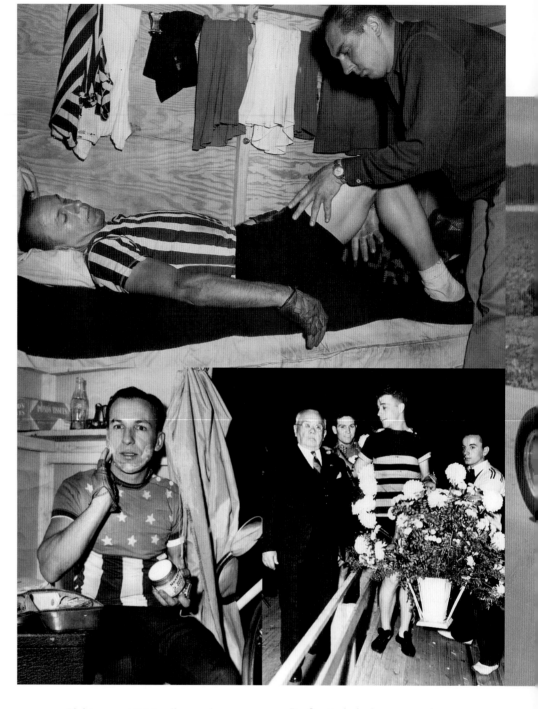

Right page: 108.9 miles an hour. Letourner delighted in taking risks, especially when it came to going faster, and called himself the "Red Devil." He helped Oscar Wastyn at the Schwinn Bicycle Company design a special motor-paced bike.

Its front chainring was so large that his tires had to be pumped up to keep the chain off the ground. One revolution of the pedals made the bicycle travel 59.67 feet. On May 17, 1941, the "Red Devil" paced behind famed car

108.9 MPH...THE RED DEVIL

racer Ronnie Householder at the wheel of a midget racing car. Householder's vehicle was equipped with a square metal shield with short flanges on the sides and top for Letourner, five feet three inches, to draft snugly behind.

They charged along a stretch of road near Bakersfield, California— startling morning commuters going to work—going 108.92 miles an hour. Verifying the record was the American Automobile Association, with its chairman

Eddie Rickenbacker, a First World War flying ace and president of Eastern Airlines. A film crew captured Letourner's world-record ride for a documentary, "Red Devil." Six months later, however, the documentary was scrapped.

POST-WAR RECOVERY

World War II put 16 million Americans in military uniforms, including young professional cyclists such as Charlie Bergna, Bill Jacoby, Cecil Yates, Charley Yaccino, and Erwin Pesek. After 1945, they were mustered out and traded their military uniforms for cycling shorts and jerseys. They tried to make up for the lost years.

VERY

Scaled-down Six-Day circuits emerged, one directed by John Baruche, and another by James "Jimmy the Whale" Proscia. Their Sixes, despite their best intentions, were low budget. Tracks were narrower and made of thin, portable wooden slabs. Yaccino once took a hard spill in Chicago and put his leg through the track.

The competitors were a mix of aging stars, such as Torchy Peden, France's Alf Letourner, Italy's gray-haired Franco Giorgetti, and returning military Veterans with a dose of velodrome rust. Promising young amateurs looked forward to the 1948 London Olympics, the first Games in twelve years. Professional cycling had ceased attracting young blood.

After the surrender of Germany and Japan in 1945, the Amateur Bicycle League of America held its national championships program for men and women in August in Chicago. They were the ABLA's first nationals after a four-year hiatus. The National Cycling Association's board tracks had all closed, sold for firewood and scrap metal. The NCA couldn't muster enough members for a national championship. The ABLA had supplanted the NCA.

Yet there were bright spots. Future Tour de France winner Hugo Koblet of Switzerland scored victories in the October 1948 Chicago Six and one held March 1949 in a New York armory. Bergna won his fifth Six-Day in January 1949 in Cleveland, paired with Cecil Yates. They were the last American team to win a Six for the rest of the century.

In 1957, Dutch promoter Chris Van Gent tried to revive American Sixes. They started in Cleveland. One hopeful joining them was Jack Heid. A New York City native, he had caught Six-Day fever as a youngster when he spotted the racers in Central Park drafting behind cars. He remarked that they made it look so easy he wanted to try it himself. After a stint in the Navy, Heid competed in the 1948 London Olympics as a sprinter on the Herne Hill Track.

Although he was eliminated early in the matched sprints, the experience whetted his appetite to improve. After the Olympics concluded and his teammates returned home, he traveled to Gent, Belgium, one of bicycle racing's unofficial capitals. In Gent, Heid lived in a house provided for him by the Belgian star Debaets.

Moving to Gent to train on the local indoor velodrome and race full-time represented a bold commitment. He was on his own financially when the economies in Belgium and surrounding countries were recovering from years of war devastation. Food essentials, including meat, sugar, and coffee, remained in such short supply that their purchase required government ration coupons, issued sparingly. Heid bought inexpensive Swiss watches in Gent and took them across the

(continued on page 199)

Facing page top left: Bill Jacoby (born 1913). Jacoby rode in Chicago's Humboldt Park in the mid-1930s, when the city boasted more than three dozen cycling clubs. He joined one sponsored by Chicago Alderman James Bowler, who had raced as a professional in the 1890s with Major Taylor.

Top right: Hanging on by tradition. Inexpensive post-War tracks such as these didn't have a guardrail. That gave spectators a clear view, with some risk of sharing their seat with a drop-in guest.

Bottom: Bedtime rush. Riders in this 1947 crash in Cleveland narrowly missed striking the bunks.

PESEK'S FALL

Pesek's fall. Pesek, shown here falling in 1948 on the narrow track in Buffalo's Memorial Auditorium, was nicknamed "Crash."

Top left: Charley Yaccino (born 1922). Yaccino, shown left, with Bill Jacoby, like many of his generation, had his career interrupted by World War II. After the war, Yaccino and Jacoby finished second together in the 1946 Chicago Six. Yaccino's last Six was 1949 in Cleveland, where he finished second with Pesek. Supporting Jacoby is fellow Chicagoan Al Stiller.

Top right: When Schwinn ruled. In 1945, Frank Schwinn provided funding from his family-owned company that played a significant role in sup-porting competitive cycling in America. Schwinn provided a five-year grant that enabled the Amateur Bicycle League of America to hold national championships until it could establish itself. Schwinn was the only American manufacturer making racing bicycles. "Schwinn Built Bicycles" written large across the top of the boards on the turn of the indoor track in New York City, circa 1947, helped keep professional racing alive.

Bottom left: Bergna in France. In 1946, Bergna raced on the roads in France. It was the era of goggles, no helmet, an aluminum bottle on handlebars, and wheels fastened by wing nuts.

Bottom right: Jack Heid (1924–1987). Heid raced on four continents and in more countries than any other American rider of his generation. Yet he had to wait till the end of his career to compete in Six-Day races. One of his last amateur races was the 1956 Tour of Somerville, America's classic fifty-mile criterium in north-central New Jersey, where he needed two hands to hold his winner's trophy.

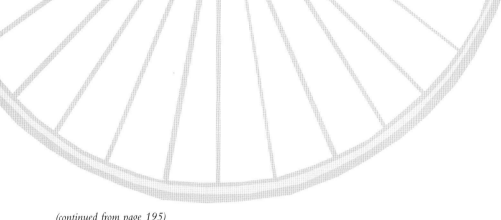

(continued from page 195)

Channel to sell in England. He competed at Herne Hill Track in London and in Manchester. Heid specialized in matched sprints. He became a favorite of audiences. The English press nicknamed him, "The Yankee Clipper."

At the 1949 world championships in Copenhagen, Heid powered to a bronze medal in the amateur sprint championship—the first world's medal for a U.S. rider since 1912. He turned professional to race on the road in Belgium and Holland. He married a Belgian woman, Julia, and they had a son. In 1951, after one race crash too many, Heid picked himself up from the muddy road, surveyed his abrasions, and decided to chuck racing for more stable employment to support his family. He returned to the United States with Julia and their son.

Competing in Six-Day races had eluded him until the promise of a domestic professional race in early 1957 lured him back to competition to fulfill his dream. Heid, who had a penchant for knocking off twenty-five chin-ups to keep in shape, turned professional again.

"The European road riders were strong and kept the pace so high, your tongue was hanging out your mouth, but it was worth it," Heid recalled of the January 1957 Cleveland Six. They included the young Dutchman Peter Post. "In Cleveland, the first night I won a new washing machine. The next night, a dryer. We kept going like that."

Chicago had hosted international Sixes since 1915. All around the city, the Walthours, McNamara, and other stars had for years enjoyed enthusiastic audiences. At the next Six-Day in Chicago, teamed with Italian Mino de Rosi, Heid had improved to finish third. Winning was the Dutch team of Post and Harm Smits. Few tickets, however, sold. It was March 1957, and Heid was there for Chicago's final Six.

"I left the Chicago Stadium with my bike and dirty laundry," Heid recalled. "All I had to show for six days of racing my heart out was a pile of dirty clothes and aching muscles. I unlocked my car, packed my bike, and drove home to Rockaway, New Jersey."

A planned event for Louisville was cancelled. This time he retired from competition for good.

This page: Joseph Magnani (1912–1975). Born in LaSalle, Illinois, Magnani grew up in Mount Clare, between the state capital in Springfield and St. Louis. In 1928, at age sixteen, he moved to southeastern France, where he joined a local amateur team. He became the only American rider to compete on the roads of Europe against Fausto Coppi, Gino Bartali, and other big names. In late 1948, Magnani returned to the United States and rode on the Six-Day circuit. He retired to work for the Schwinn Bicycle Company, where he designed the Paramount road bicycle. Through 1972, he assembled all of Schwinn's Paramount tandem, track, and road bikes.

Nostalgia led to the mounting of a campaign in September 1961 to revive Six-Day racing in Madison Square Garden. Alf Letourner visited Paris on behalf of the Garden's management and signed up world champions Rudi Altig of Germany and Oscar Plattner of Switzerland, Tour de France stage winner Brian Robinson of England, and others to compose an international field as classy as any in the Garden.

Preceding page spread:

Swansong Garden Six-Day

race. In the 1961 edition,

Swiss world champion sprint-

er Oscar Plattner lays a hand

on Erwin Pesek, held by

retired 1930s track pro Louis

Watson of Brooklyn. Plattner

won with Armin Von Buren.

The tradition of a celebrity

firing the starting pistol

went to the buxom television

comedian known as Dagmar

(born Virginia Ruth Egnor).

The Garden's Six turned out

to be the end of the line

for New York's lineage.

Nevertheless, this was the

75th running of the New

York Six-Day race.

Also in the thirty-rider mix was a cadre of Americans. Among them were Chicago's Pesek and Al Stiller, Pat Murphy of Delhi, Ontario, and Ted Smith of Buffalo. The entertainment weekly *Variety* announced: "6-Day Bike Race, Back after 22 Years, Recalls Prohibition's Razzle-Dazzle."

Some old hands directed the event. Goullet worked as chief referee, with Charles Bergna as his assistant. Yet construction of the pine saucer fell behind schedule. Thousands of fans waited several hours on Friday evening, September 22, before demanding refunds and walking out. The cyclists eventually were called to the start line. As professionals, they put on a show of speed and graceful bike handling around the banked turns.

"The quality of the riders made it a first-class race," remarked Lawrence Herman, of Washington, D.C., who witnessed the race. "I've never seen anything like it. On the final night, there were 10,000 spectators. Many were people who remembered the Garden's old Six-Day races. At that time, New York City had a great many people from Western Europe. There were a lot of Italians in the crowd, great enthusiasm."

The Swiss team of Plattner and Armin Von Buren won. None of the Americans completed the event.

Although the final night's gate enjoyed a rally, total receipts fell short of expectations. American Six-Day racing had ended in the same oblivion as Prohibition. The 1961

Garden Six was New York City's 75th and final edition. The Europeans went home, practically taking Six-Day racing with them.

Pesek packed his two racing bicycles in their travel box and returned to Chicago. He cleaned his frames, greased the axles, put new tires on the rims. He nested his bicycle frames, wheels, and handlebars back in their box, ready for the next Six-Day. No call came. His bicycles remain boxed and race-ready.

He and others of his generation grew up learning about cycling heroes such as the Walthours, Letourner, and Goullet. Pesek wanted to take his place in the pantheon of cycling stars. Yet he came of age in time to witness the sport's downward spiral.

What confronted Pesek had started years earlier. In 1926, Goullet, recently retired, liked going with Tex Rickard to watch New York Giants football games. Goullet realized he had an opportunity. He asked Chapman to lease him the Newark Velodrome after Labor Day. Chapman asked what Goullet had in mind. Goullet cheerfully explained that he wanted to take advantage of the velodrome's grandstand and bleachers surrounding the grassy infield. He planned to install goal posts and mark up the field for football games.

Chapman had grown up in a log cabin with a dirt floor on a farm in College Park, Georgia, and rose through cycling promotions to

(continued on page 205)

Top: Ted Smith (1928–1992). In 1945, Ted Smith of Buffalo had just turned eighteen when he won the national Amateur Bicycle League of America championship in Chicago. He won two more titles and competed in the 1948 London Olympics. Returning home, he accepted a contract for $25,000 to turn professional and race Sixes, beginning in Buffalo. He moved to Belgium to compete in road races until he was drafted in 1952 into the Army. Smith turned professional for the second time to ride in the Garden's 1961 Six-Day revival, paired with Pat Murphy.

Bottom: After winning all the best trophies as an amateur, Ted Smith turned professional to ride Six-Day races.

((PAT MURPHY))

Born 1933. One of the big names
of North American racing in the
1950s, Pat Murphy grew up in

participated in the 1956
Melbourne Olympics. Murphy
represented Canada at the 1958

Reunion. Bobby Walthour Jr., second from left, visited the 1961 Garden Six with retired professionals Carl Hanbacker, on the far left, Frank Cavanaugh (resting his hand on the shoulder of Louis Watson), Fred Taylor, and William Beck.

(continued from page 202)

become a Georgia land baron. Football had a raffish underworld reputation. He rejected Goullet's request.

"Chapman said football was for high school kids and college boys," Goullet recalled. "He said that nobody would ever pay to watch professional football."

Chapman had wanted to keep running his programs the same way. He couldn't foresee that football would soar to prominence—no more than today's National Football League fans could imagine a time when their sport amounted to a poor relation to Six-Day races. Nor could he anticipate that long-distance travel would change from

trains to commercial airlines. That transformation involved his beloved Velodrome Farm. It was paved over for jet runways and terminals and became Atlanta's Hartsfield International Airport, one of the world's busiest airports.

But even in Europe in the 1960s, the appeal of Six-Day racing was eroding. The sport's balance of power tipped to road racing. During the first years of the Tour de France, *L'Auto* publisher Henri Desgrange had presses working around the clock daily to meet booming demand for race coverage. World War I stopped his event for five years. When Desgrange resumed his Tour in 1919, he

increased it to fifteen days. He capitalized on the newspaper's yellow newsprint by clothing the race leader in a matching yellow jersey. By 1927, he limited his event to three weeks because that was all his presses could bear. World War II interrupted the Tour for seven years. In 1945 *L'Auto* changed its name to *L'Equipe*, and the Tour de France, resumed in 1947, has grown into a major French institution.

Other newspapers put on national tours, such as Italy's Giro d'Italia and Spain's Vuelta á España. They and other road races all increased in prestige as radio broadcasts and then television coverage found a younger and growing audience.

EXPORTED TO EUROPE

A seismic shift occurred in American popular culture. Television broadcasts propelled major league baseball, basketball, and football into households from coast to coast. Bicycle racing, once an American sports tradition, diminished to a subculture of hardy amateurs, largely ignored by the press and the general public.

PORTED

In the 1960s, the Amateur Bicycle League of America issued licenses to about 900 men and 100 women. The career goal for many amounted to making the Olympic cycling team, which was open only to men. Those who succeeded received a complimentary Schwinn Paramount. The domestic bicycle racing diet consisted chiefly of circuit races of up to fifty miles around loops in remote industrial parks or more accessible downtown streets such as those in Somerville, New Jersey, or Nevada City, California.

Information circulated in cycling's subculture mostly by word of mouth. In Berkeley, California, Peter Rich started a newsletter with race results and training tips, typed on a manual typewriter and reproduced by hand-cranking a mimeograph machine in the back of his bicycle shop, Velo-Sport. First published as the *Northern California Cycling Association Newsletter*, his publication would eventually became *Bicycling Magazine*.

Jack Simes III, a third-generation racer and three-time Olympian from Closter, New Jersey, grew up hearing about the glory days of cycling from his father and grandfather, both former professionals. Simes also learned about tactics and big-time racers from Heid, who had been trained by Jackie Simes II. Young Jack set national records for the kilometer and fifty miles. After Simes III won a silver medal in the kilometer at the 1968 world track championships in

Montevideo, Uruguay, he turned professional and traveled to Europe to race Sixes. Simes prevailed upon Heid for contacts in Belgium to introduce him to track promoters.

Without the benefit of corporate sponsorship, and on his own to make travel arrangements, Simes coped with different languages and currencies. Moreover, it took weeks for him to adjust to different water, diet, weather, and chilly buildings that still lacked central heating.

John Vande Velde of Chicago also came from a cycling family. He won three national individual pursuit championships and took a bronze medal in the Pan American Games. After he competed in the 1972 Munich Olympics, he joined Simes on the Six-Day circuit.

The American team paid their dues and earned respect. Simes and Vande Velde did best in North America, with top-three finishes in four Sixes in Montreal, Los Angeles, and Detroit. Yet, however well they performed, they did so in front of empty seats. On this side of the Atlantic, Sixes suffered as a subcategory of a minor sport.

Six-Day racing continued on stubbornly in some European cities. The format featured frequent sprints for points in the afternoons through the early-morning hours, augmented by hard-driving music on powerful sound systems to keep the audience pumped up.

Marty Nothstein, of Allentown, Pennsylvania, grew up racing on Friday nights on the nearby

Lehigh County Velodrome, where Simes III had developed race programs. Nothstein learned skills on the outdoor cement velodrome and rose within the U.S. Cycling Federation, successor to the Amateur Bicycle League of America. The USCF now has its headquarters at the U.S. Olympic Training Center in Colorado Springs and operates with the help of corporate sponsorships. Nothstein traveled worldwide as a member of the USCF national team and competed against top international talent.

Nothstein moved up cycling's ranks. He won a string of thirty-four national track championships, making him the latter-day Frank Kramer. At the 1994 world championships in Palermo, Italy, he won the sprint title. His victory was the first in the men's professional sprint since Kramer's, eighty-two years earlier. He also won a second world championship in the Keirin, a track event featuring a group of cyclists drafting at speed behind a motorcycle that peels off with 2.5 laps remaining to let them battle to the end.

At the 1996 Atlanta Olympics, Nothstein was widely considered a favorite to win gold in the matched sprints against the defending champion, Germany's Jens Fiedler. But Fiedler edged out Nothstein in two straight matches to win. Nothstein went home with a silver medal.

(continued on page 211)

Top: View from the bridge. Walking from the bridge to the infield of the 1972 Montreal Six was a smoky experience.

Left: Jack Simes III (born 1942). America's No. 1 cyclist of the 1960s, when amateur racing ruled, Simes took the unusual step of traveling frequently, and at his own expense, to compete in Europe. He rode in ten Six-Day races. After he retired, Simes helped build professional racing in the United States. Among his accomplishments were updating the National Cycling Association to the U.S. Professional Racing Organization (USPRO), now part of USA Cycling, and organizing the first sprint programs at the Lehigh County Velodrome, the country's most successful outdoor velodrome.

Marty Nothstein, top, takes over from Ryan Simes Oelkers in a Madison race. Their victory at the March 2002 Moscow Six-Day race marked the first U.S. team victory since Charlie Bergna and Cecil Yates in 1949 in Cleveland— and one of American cycling's brightest moments.

John Vande Velde (born 1949). Hearing stories from his Belgian relatives of professional racing while growing up in Chicago, Vande Velde sought to become a professional and compete in Six-Day races in Europe after the 1972 Munich Olympics. His daughter Marisa Vande Velde won national track championships and rode on the U.S. Cycling Federation national team. His son Christian Vande Velde rode on the 1999 U.S. Postal Services Team to support Lance Armstrong in winning his first Tour de France.

(continued from page 202)

For the next four years, Nothstein worked out four to six hours daily, training on the Lehigh Valley Velodrome, lifting weights in the gym and racing in world-class meets. In the weight room, he loaded up the weight bar with 270 pounds, put it on his shoulders, and did squats until the repetitions made him feel dizzy and he rushed to the bucket that hc kept there to throw up in. He bulked up his six-foot, two-inches to 215 pounds with thirty-inch thighs. Every training ride, weight workout, and sit-up he did for his goal of winning the gold at the 2000 Sydney Olympics.

When he faced Fiedler in a semi-final heat in Sydney, Nothstein dominated to win in two straight matches. Fiedler had to settle for a bronze medal. Nothstein went on to win the Olympic gold. He had validated himself as the fastest cyclist in the world. Yet track racing offered little opportunity for the Olympic gold medalist looking to cash in on his talents. All that remained was Europe's Six-Day winter circuit.

"The racing was so fast and went on for hour after hour—I was starting out as a raw beginner," Nothstein said. "At this point in my career, the experience was very humbling."

As a Six-Day novice at age thirty, Nothstein concentrated on learning his new discipline. After the rigors of his first season on the indoor Sixes, he lost ten pounds. In early 2002 he persuaded Ryan Simes Oelkers, the nephew of Simes III, to join him. In March of that year, Nothstein and Oelkers won the Moscow Six—the first American team victory since Bergna and Yates in 1949 in Cleveland.

From Harry Etherington to Marty Nothstein, all have shared the same passion to ride fast. That urge made cycling change and grow. In the 1960s, kids in California riding small bikes with seats jacked up high and holding onto straight handlebars created BMX racing. Now on most weekends thousands of BMX racers careen in competitions around tight turns on dirt tracks and jump their bikes over ramps and mounds. In the late 1970s, in Marin County, California, enthusiasts pedaling heavy ballooned-tired bikes on fire trails created mountain bike racing. Cross-country mountain bike racing made its debut as an Olympic sport for men and women at the Atlanta Olympics.

The Nothstein-Oelkers's victory in Moscow completed a circle of Americans in Six-Day races. Today, there are about ten Sixes, rambunctiously popular, in German, Belgium, and Dutch cities. They include Berlin, where demand for tickets is so high that they sell out a year in advance. Riders whirling around the pine saucer follow the wheel marks of MacFarland and Moran. Two-rider team races remain popular in track competitions of various distances, such as 150-laps, and are known worldwide as Madisons.

((GERMANY))

Six-Day racing has
continued to thrive
to this day in some
European cities. This
1974 photo shows
the action during a
Six-Day race in
Muenster, Germany.

(ACKNOWLEDGEMENTS)

The authors wish to thank the U.S. Bicycling Hall of Fame (www.usbhof.com), especially curator Vince Menci, for opening its extensive archives to us and sharing what he has learned about the Six-Day riders. Over the years, Vince has shaken hands with more American cycling heroes than anyone else.

We would also like to thank Lorne Shields (vintage-antique2@rogers.com) for generously making his archival collection available, including Harry Etherington's scrapbook; Stever Davis of Corbis, for permission to use several Corbis images; and the families of Ed Kelty, Jr. and Herb Kelty, for the frontspiece photo.

Richard Schwinn, one of American cycling's natural resources and a fourth-generation frame builder at Waterford Precision Cycles (www.waterfordbikes.com), brought the three of us together for this project.

I am also grateful to Ray and Louise Blum for inspiration, Ari de Wilde for insights into early collegiate racing, Jere Cunningham for his energetic support, Claire Landis-Tyson for organizing the video interviews, and members of the National Capital Velo Club of Washington, D.C., and Rolling Bay Wheelmen of the Seattle area for patiently listening to our stories about the Six-Day racers.

For background on John M. Chapman, special thanks to Charlotte S. Winsness of Pine Mountain Valley, Georgia who serves as family historian and researched the Georgia Archives for property deeds on microfilm and other family genealogy. Also special thanks for information on Iver Lawson's background in Sweden from Gunnar Svartengren. A note of appreciation goes to Arthur LeMond, Greg LeMond's paternal grandfather, for information about his early years living in Newark and his elder cousin, the trainer Fred Bullivant.

Many other people shared scrapbooks, recollections, and otherwise lent us support. They include Sammy Gastman and his granddaughter Nancy Jennis Olds, Bill and Francis Brennan, Frank and Ella Bartell, Jerry and Bea Rodman, Norman and Betty Hill and the Hill family, Bill and Muriel Jacoby, Frank and Joe Turano, Bill and Edna Honeman, Ted Ernst Jr., Oscar and Adolph Juner, Clem Skeehan, Joe Neville, Betty Carr, Eddy Smith and family, Buck Peacock, Brett Horton, Alfred Goulette, John Baron, Ted Harper, Lou MacPherson, Michael Gabriel, Morris and Hazel Robinson, Lorne Atkinson, Charlie Bergna, Doris Kopsky Mueller, Don Hester, Joe Cirone, Tom and Linda Spain, David and Iris Burnett, Eddie Testa, Don Wares, Sterling and Patricia Wise, Marty Epstein, Erv Pesek, Willy Rabel, Frank and Margaret Mihlon, Jack and Julia Heid, Jackie Simes II and Jack Simes III, Joan and Bobby Walthour III, Bobby Walthour IV, Bruce Colvin, Andy Taus, Henry "Hank" Banta, Keith Kingbay, Myron Lehtman, Harry Hopkins, Ted Smith, Pete Swan, Al Hatos, and Robert George.

Peter Joffre Nye has written five books, including *Hearts of Lions: The History of American Bicycle Racing*, and *The Lance Armstrong Performance Program*, by Lance and his long-time coach Chris Carmichael. As a graduate student at the London School of Economics, Nye competed for the Norwood Paragon Cycle Club. For one year, he held the Southern Counties Cycling Federation's Tacagni Cup, which dates back to 1876, something that deepened his appreciation of cycling history and tradition.

For the last thirty years, he has worked as a journalist and editor in Washington, DC. He also serves as an historical advisor to the U.S. Cycling Hall of Fame.

Jeff Groman is known nationally for his collection of historic cycling photographs. He has operated bicycle shops in the Seattle, Washington, area for over twenty years. His current shop is on Bainbridge Island, near Seattle. He is also the curator of a museum of cycling history.

Mark Tyson grew up in Ohio and learned about cycling history from some of the local old-timers. He is a graduate of Bowling Green State University, where he studied history and TV production. He is president of Main Street Production in Colorado Springs, Colorado.

(BIBLIOGRAPHY)

BOOKS

Eliot Asinof. *Eight Men Out: The Black Sox and the 1919 World Series.* New York: Henry Holt, 1963.

Peter Arnold. *History of Boxing.* Secaucus, N.J.: Chartwell Books, 1985.

William A. Brady. *Showman: My Life Story.* New York: E.P. Dutton & Co., 1937.

Harry Van Den Bremt and René Jacobs. *VeloPlus.* Dendermonde, Belgium: Het Nieuwsblad, 1985.

Chronicle of America. New York: Dorling Kindersley, 1995.

Joseph Durso. *Madison Square Garden: 100 Years of History.* New York: Simon and Schuster, 1979.

Otto Eisele. *Cycling Almanac.* New York: published by the author, 1950; 1951; 1952; 1953; 1954.

F. Scott Fitzgerald. *The Crack-Up*, Edited by Edmund Wilson. New York: New Directions, 1993.

—. *The Short Stories of F. Scott Fitzgerald: A New Collection, Edited by Matthew J. Broccoli.* New York: Charles Scribner's Sons, 1989.

Michael C. Gabriele. *The Nutley Velodrome: A History of the Legendary Cycling Mecca*, 1983.

Neal Gabler. *An Empire of Their Own: How the Jews Invented Hollywood.* New York: Anchor Books, 1989.

Barbara George. *Ten Years of Championship Bicycle Racing: 1972–1981.* Brattleboro, Vt.: Velo-News, 1983.

Leslie Halliwell. *Halliwell's Film Guide*, 7th. Ed. New York: Harper & Row, 1989.

Ted Harper. *Six Days of Madness.* Stroud, Ontario, Canada: Pacesetter Press, 1993.

William A. Harper. *How You Played the Game: The Life of Grantland Rice.* Columbia, Missouri: University of Missouri Press, 1999.

Ernest Hemingway. *A Moveable Feast.* New York: Charles Scribner's Sons, 1964.

David V. Herlihy. *Bicycle: The History.* New Haven: Yale University Press, 2004.

Roger De Maertelaere. *De Mannen van de Nacht, 100 Jaar Zesdaagsen.* Eeklo, Belgium: Eekloonaar, 2000.

Peter Nye. *Hearts of Lions: The History of American Bicycle Racing.* New York: W.W. Norton, 1988.

—. *The Cyclist's Sourcebook.* New York: Perigee Books, 1991.

USA Cycling 75th Anniverary: The Saga of Struggle, Courage, and Cycling Glory. Salem, Mass.: Arena Advertising, 1998.

Arthur Judson Palmer. *Riding High: The Century of the Bicycle.* New York: E.P. Dutton & Co., 1956.

Constance Rosenblum, *Gold Digger: the Outrageous Life and Times of Peggy Hopkins Joyce* New York: Metropolitan Books/Henry Holt & Company, 2000.

Ari de Wilde. "*Too Fast for Their Own Good: A History of Collegiate Cycling*," thesis presented to the faculty of the Department of History, Bates College, Lewiston, Maine, 2004.

James Thurber. *The Years with Ross.* Boston: Little, Brown & Company, 1957.

SELECTED PERIODICAL ARTICLES

Harvey Araton. "One More Lap, with Feeling, for American." *The New York Times*, September 21, 2000.

Walter Bardgett. "Champion Kramer Says Farewell." *Motorcycle and Bicycle Illustrated*, August 1922.

—. "On the Bell Lap." *American Bicyclists and Motorcyclist*, April 1947; July 1947.; October 1947.

Victor Breyer. "And What About the N.C.A.?" *American Bicyclists and Motorcyclist*, February 1945.

Stuart Bentstead. " 'The Kid Who Went to Town," *The Sporting Cyclist*, January 1960.

Frank M. Blunk. "Capacity Crowd Is Due at Finale: But New Generation Seems Bored by Song of Wheels as Time Backpedals." *The New York Times*, September 28, 1961

W.D. Bratz. "Lawson to Ride No More: Salt Lake Star Who Has Often Startled Cycling World Announces Retirement from Game." From Lawson's scrapbook, about November 1916.

William Briody. "Bike Promoters Face Heavy Loss." *The New York Times*, September 24, 1961.

Dave Chauner. "Back in the Early 1900s, Bicycling Was Big and Frank Kramer Was King." *Sports Illustrated*, May 15, 1984.

Harold Conrad. "6-Day Bike Race, Back After 22 Years, Recalls Prohibition's Razzle-Dazzle." *Variety* (Hollywood, California), August 23, 1961.

Raymond Dickow. "Silent 'Sixes' of the States." *Sporting Cyclist*, November 1960.

Bert Dodge. "Diagnosing Kramer and Spencer." *Motorcycle and Bicycle Illustrated*, September 16, 1917.

"For Six Days," *Fortune* (New York City), March 1935.

G.A. Falzer. "Bike Track Gone, Riders Linger in Nutley." Scrapbook, 1945.

Nat Fleischer. "Veterans Hark Back to Miller, Waller, McFarland." About 1915, from Walthour III scrapbook.

Paul Gallico. "Another Advertisement." *The New York Daily News*, March 5, 1928.

Russ Gatlin. "The Wooden Wonders." *Automobile Quarterly*, Vol. IX, No. 3, Spring 1971, pp. 256–265.

William Hennigan. "Brocco and Goullet Steal Lap and Win in Sensational Finish." *The New York World*, December 11, 1921.

"Horan an MSG Fixture as Usher, 6-Day Biker" *Long Island Press*, September 10, 1972.

Joe Hovis. "National Cycling Review." *The Staten Island Transcript*, November 30, 1959.

—. "Old Timers' Night." *The Staten Island Transcript*, November 20, 1959.

Raymond Hull. "Reggie McNamara: Iron Knight of the Bike World." *The Arena and Strength*, December 1934.

Paul W. Kearney. "The Human Squirrel Cage." *Esquire*, September 1937.

R.F. Kelsey. "Cycling Year of 1914 Brightest in Many." *The Bicycling World and Motorcycle Review*, January 5, 1915.

John Kieran. "Sports of the Times." *The New York Times*, March 6, 1927.

Al Laney. "Boy Cyclists Don't Know 'Big Steve,' But All East Orange Knows Kramer: Greatest of All Bicycle Riders, Veteran of 20's in Jersey Job at 66." *Newark Evening News*, December 24, 1946.

Francine Latil. "Speed Demon." *The Ride*, Issue 119, 2004.

Rene de Latour. "The Other MacNamara," *Sporting Cyclist*, November 1967.

"Victoire de Lawson a Berlin." August 21, 1904 dateline from Berlin, in Iver Lawson's scrapbook.

"Former Champion talks of Iver Lawson's First Appearance and Other Interesting Reminiscences." From Lawson's scrapbook.

Frank Litsky. "Cyclist Travels in Fastest Circles." *The New York Times*, July 18, 1996.

—. "After an Early Breakaway, the Stamina to Keep Going." August 4, 2003.

J.J. Mahar. "Australian Supreme in America." From scrapbook of Harris Horder.

Anthony Marenghi. "Kramer Quits 'Drome Post; Hill Made Referee." *Newark Ledger*, March 12, 1938.

—. "Evel Is No Alfred Letourner." *Newark Evening News*. January 11, 1975.

Harry Mendel. "Frank Kramer's Life Story." *Motor Cycle Illustrated*. December 30, 1916; January 6, 1916; January 20, 1916; January 27, 1916; February 3, 1916; February 10, 1916; February 17, 1916; February 24, 1916; March 9, 1916; March 16, ; March 23, 1916; March 30, 1916; April 6, ; April 13; April 17, 1916; May 4, 1916; May 11, ; May 25, 1916.

—. "History of the Garden Bike Races: Starting in 1891 on High Wheels Cyclists Competed in 58 International

Grinds." Official Program, 59th International 6-Day Bike Race, Dec. 1 to 7, 1935, Madison Square Garden.

Reggie McNamara. "The Race Is To the Swift—Sometimes." Unpublished manuscript in Jeff Groman collection.

—. "Half a Million Miles." *Bicycling*, September-October 1946.

Charles Meinert. "Six-Day Bicycle Races in Madison Square Garden During the 1890s, Part I." *The Wheelmen*, No. 53, February, 1999.

—. "Six-Day Bicycle Races in Madison Square Garden During the 1890s, Part II." No. 54, May 1999.

"Man Who Organized the First Six-Days' Bicycle Race." *Bicycling News*, September 15, 1938.

Kip Mikler. "Back in the Spotlight: Nothstein Scores His Biggest Win Yet in New York." *VeloNews,* September 8, 2003.

Joseph C. Nichols. "Six-Day Bike Race Back at Garden Tonight After 22 Years." *The New York Times*. September 22, 1961.

Peter Nye. "Champion from Down Under Was Tops in America." *Cycling USA*, November 1994.

—. "Glory Days." *Cycling USA*, October 1994.

—. "The Kid Who Caught Six-Day Fever." *Winning*, March 20, 1985.

—. "From Zimmerman to Nothstein." *VeloNews*, December 16, 1996.

—. "1930s Olympian Sinibaldi Now Rides the Masters Nationals." *VeloNews*, July 15, 1996.

—. "A Junior's Life in the '50s: Ruesing's Cycling Medals Earned Admission to Harvard." *VeloNews*, February 5, 1996.

—. "Kramer Was On Top of the World." *VeloNews*, January 15, 1996.

—. "One of the Bigger Wheels: Alf Goullet, Still Spry at 99, Was Cycling's Darling in the Six-Day Races of the 1920s." *Sports Illustrated*, November 12, 1990.

—. "Hill Raced with the Stars." *VeloNews*, September 18, 1995.

—. "Chicago's Six-Day Stadium Falls to Wrecker's Ball." *VeloNews*, April 24, 1996.

—. "Brennan's Held 70 Years of Memories." *VeloNews*, November 7, 1994.

—. "Honeman Wore First Stars and Stripes Jersey." *VeloNews*, June 27, 1994.

—. "Kramer Remembered at Hall of Fame." *VeloNews*, March 21, 1994.

—. "World Championships, Born in Chicago, Celebrate Centenary." *VeloNews*, August 30, 1993.

—. "The Early Days of Bike (and Auto) Racing: How Henry Ford Hitched His Career to Tom Cooper, the Cycling Phenom of 1895." *VeloNews*, May 27, 1996.

—. "Bob Spears: The Tallest Sprint Champ." *VeloNews*, June 14, 1993.

—. "Murphy Challenged the Europeans in the 1950s." *VeloNews*, January 20, 1992.

—. "American Classics: Races that Have Spanned the Decades." *Cycling USA*, October/November 1999.

—. "Victor Hopkins: Earlier Olympian Pedals from Hometown to Olympic Trials." *Cycling USA*, May 1992.

—. "Bobby Walthour: One of America's Greatest." *Cycling USA*, March 1995.

—. "Reggie McNamara: Original Ironman on Wheels." *Cycling USA*, August 1994.

—. "Ultimate Fashion Statement Set at 1974 Road National Championship." *Cycling USA*, July 1994.

—. "Bell's Start in PanAm Kilo One of Most Controversial in History." *Cycling USA*, October 1991.

—. "Joseph Magnani: America's Forgotten Pioneer." *Bicyclist Magazine*. February 1998.

—. "Our Winningest Olympic Cyclist." *Bicycle Guide*, August 1996.

—. "NYAC's Century of World Champion Cyclists Circle is Unbroken." *The Winged Foot*, February 1995.

—. "100 Years of Schwinn: The Family Business that Kept U.S. Cycling Rolling." *Bicycle Guide*, November 1995.

—. "Newark, N.J., Started a National Cycling Tradition." *The Ride*, Issue 109, 2003.

—. "Grampa LeMond." *Spokes*, June 1992.

"Origin of Six Day Races: Eck Talks of the Early Grinds and of the Men Who Made Them Possible." *The Bicycling World*, December 26, 1903.

Willie Ratner. "Horder, Australian Star, Winner of Sprint Title: Horder's Career Started When He Was Only Twelve." *Newark Evening News*. Horder scrapbook.

—. "John M. Chapman." April 22, 1915.

—. Twenty Pro Bicycle Riders Are Suspended by Karmer." *Newark Evening News*, undated, about 1928, from Walthour III scrapbook.

—. " 'How It Feels to Promote Outlaw Race' by H. Brennan." Newark Evening News, undated, about 1928, from Walthour III scrapbook.

—. "Cyclists Assail Head of N.C.A. as High-Handed. *Newark Evening News*, December 22, 1932.

—. "Requiem for a 'Fighter': Death of Neville Stirs Memories of 6-Day Races." *Newark Evening News*. Undated, from scrapbook.

—. "Chapman Signs Long Contract As Garden 6-Day Race Manager." *Newark Evening News*. February 18, 1930

—. "What Happened to Bike Racing?" *Newark Evening News*. April 10, 1955.

Bob Ottum. "Lure of the Wild White Noise." *Sports Illustrated*, September 14, 1964.

Rod Reed. "These Six-Day Bike Racers—Do They Eat! Steaks, Stews, Soups, Eggs, Rice, Etc., Etc." *Buffalo Times*, January 23, 1934.

Paul Reinhard. "Nothstein in Awe of Local Reception." *Allentown Morning Call*. October 18, 2000.

Grantland Rice. "The King Maker: Tex Rickard has made himself the Warwick of the Heavyweight Game." *Colliers*. November 13, 1926.

Robert L. Ripley. "Goullet: The Human Motorcycle." *The New York Globe*, November 24, 1914.

Andrew Ritchie. "The Beginnings of Trans-Atlantic Bicycle Racing: Harry Etherington and the Anglo-French Team in America, 1879–80." *International Journal of the History of Sport*, Vol. 15, No. 3, Dec. 1998.

Damon Runyon. "Sport Editorial: 'Ol' Al' Goullet." *New York American*, December 12, 1921.

—. "Alfred the Great." Race program for the March 1923 Madison Square Garden Six-Day.

Walter Ryan. "6-Day Whirlers Spinning: Fifteen Teams Get Under Way in 44th International Grind." *The New York Daily News*, March 5, 1928.

Bill Slocum. "Race Is Rule by Dictator, Says Horder." *New York American*, November 3, 1932.

Paul Taylor. "A Ride to Redemption: The Freewheeling Drama of Match Sprint Cycling Was on Full Display When Marty Nothstein Went Tire-To-Tire With His Old Nemesis." *Sports Illustrated*, October 18, 2000.

John Wilcockson. "Alf Goullet at 100: A Century of Memories from the Six-Day 'King'." *VeloNews*, April 22, 1991.

(ILLUSTRATION CREDITS)

Illustrations used are from the collections of Jeff Groman, Mark Tyson and/or Peter Joffre Nye except as listed below.

Ed Kelty, Jr. collection: pp. 2–3; 186–187

U.S. Bicycling Hall of Fame collection: pp. 6; 29; 32-33; 37 right; 39; 40 top right and bottom; 41; 42; 45; 46 top; 47 bottom; 48; 51; 52; 54; 56; 57; 58; 59; 63; 65; 66; 69; 70; 71 left and right; 73; 74 bottom; 75; 79; 80; 84; 86; 89; 94; 97 bottom; 103; 104 insert; 110; 111 bottom; 112; 114-115; 116; 117; 118 top; 119 left; 128 top; 136; 138; 139; 142; 144; 153; 155; 156; 157; 162; 165; 166; 172; 175 top; 178; 180; "184; 190 right 192; 194 top right and bottom; 198 top right and bottom right; 203 top and bottom; 205

Brennan Family collection: p. 97 top

Lorne Shields collection: p. 25 top left and top center

Rob van der Plas collection: pp. 25 top right; 36 top; 178; 212–213

Buck Peacock collection: pp. 25 bottom; 26–27

Bobby Walthour III collection: pp. 28; 36 bottom; 37 left; 109; 120; 122; 123; 124; 125; 126; 127; 129 bottom; 135; 145

Shelly & Brett Horton/The Horton collection: pp. 35; 40 top left

Harry Hopkins collection: pp. 71 center; 74; 93 bottom right; 119 right

Erwin Pesek collection: pp. 100; 102; 196–197; 200

Mike DeFilippo collection: p. 167

Charlie Bergna collection: pp. 174; 187 bottom; 188; 189; 190 top and bottom left; 198 bottom left

Lori McGowan collection: p. 182

Bill Jacoby collection: pp. 194 top left; 198 top left

Rudy Magnani collection: p. 199

Jack Simes III collection: p. 210

Pat Murphy collection: p. 204

Robert George: pp. 206; 209; 211

Corbis: pp. 46 bottom; 47 top; p. 62 middle and bottom; 78; 170; 175 bottom

(INDEX)

A

Allen, Gracie, 148
Altig, Rudi, 201
Amateur Bicycle League of
    America (ABLA), 72, 249, 208
American Cycling Association
    (ACA), 55
Atlantic City Velodrome, 165
Audy, Jules, 164, 166–167
Australia, 46

B

Bailey, Blanche, "Daisy," 43–44
Bardgett, Walter, 40, 97
Barrymore, John, 61
Bartell, Frank, 118–121, 158
    and speed record, 158
baseball, 10
bathrobes, as warm-up suits, 71
Bedard, Raymond, 184, 186
Belloni, Gaetano, 81
Bergna, Charlie, 173, 186–187,
    189–190, 193
    and accident, 174–175
    as road racer, 198
    and massage, 190
    on training ride, 188–189
Berlin, 50
Bicycling Hall of Fame, 182
    and McNamara, 182
"Black Sox" scandal, 9, 132,
    137–138
Black Tuesday, 149
Bollaert, Archie, 173
Bowler, James, Chicago
    alderman, 195
boxing, 46
Brady, Billy, 28
Brennan, Bill, 97
    and food at Six-Day races, 114
Brennan, John, "Pop," 97, 172–173

Brocco, Maurice, 70
budget, of Chapman's Six-Day
    races, 149
Bullivant, Fred, 85–91, 144,
    173–174, 183
    and Walthour Jr., 122, 127
bunks, 80, 102, 194
Burns, George, 148
Butler, Nat, 38–39

C

Cann, Billie, 24–25
Cantor, Eddie, 152–153
Caruso, Enrico, 61
Cavanagh, Frank, 205
Chapman, John M.,
    43–47, 50, 55,
    62–64, 72, 95, 127,
    132, 136–149,
    171–173, 202–205
    and American Cycling
        Association (ACA), 55
    and budget, 149
    and dealings with riders,
        62–64, 95
    and expansion of Six-Day
        racing, 46, 50, 149
    and Jimmy Walthour, Jr., 132
    and Mendel, 171
    and National Cycling
        Association (NCA), 72
    and nickname "Czar," 137
    and prize money, 138
    and retirement, 127, 147
    and revising Six-Day
        format, 62
    and ticket prices, 149
    and MacFarland at Madison
        Square Garden, 55
    and Spencer, 143–144

and World Championships, 50
Chicago Stadium, 16
Clark, Jackie, 50, 52, 54, 118
    and eating, 118
Cook, Bill, 170, 173
Coolidge, President Calvin, 127
Cooper, Jackie, 151
Corbett, "Gentleman Jim," 28
"Crash," as nickname for Pesek,
    197
crashes, 82–91, 194–195, 197
Crossley, Alfred, 133, 164, 189
    and Jimmy Walthour, Jr., 189
Cugnot, Jean, 138
cycling periodicals, 44
"Cycling Czar," see Chapman,
    John, M.

D

Debaets, Gerard, 90, 91, 93,
    139, 139
DeFilippo, Mike, 87, 164, 167, 169
    and Bullivant, 87
    and Kramer, 164–169
de Latour, René, 87, 183
    and McNamara, 87, 183
    and drugs, 87
Dempsey, Harry/Jack, 50, 68,
    72, 144
    as starter, 72
    and name change, 68
Depression, 149, 155, 173
Desgrange, Henri, 205
Didriksen, Babe, 166–167
Downing, Hardy, 44
Drobach, Pete, 84
drugs, 83–91
Duelberg, Franz, 132, 156–157
Dupré, Victor, 55
Durante, 150

E

"eagle soup" (cocaine drinks), 87
Eck, Tom, 24–25, 30–31
  and track construction, 102
Egg, Oscar, 52, 69, 71
Elder, Lew, 119
Ellegaard, Thorvald, 35
Etherington, Harry, 24–25
Europe, post-war, 205–213

F

Fairbanks, Douglas, 61
Fenn, William Sr., 29
Fiedler, Jens, 208, 211
fire, at Newark Velodrome, 193
"Flappers," 68
Fogler, Joe, 54–55, 78
food, at six-day races, 113–119
Fortune Magazine, 67–68
Freedman, Howard, cartoonist, 75
Friol, Emile, 50

G

Gadou, Laurent, 119
Gallico, Paul, 10
Garrison, Leroy, 156–157
Gastman, Sammy, 71, 114, 119
  and eating, 114
Germany, post-war Six-Day
  racing, 211–213
"Giants of the Velodrome,"
  photo, 74–75
Giorgetti, Franco, 139
"Good Old Days," cartoon, 28
Goosens, Alfonse, 139, 141–142
Gordon, Morrie, 118
Goullett, Alf, 13, 46–47, 53,
  55, 68, 71, 78, 108–109,
  111, 202
  and Chapman, 46
  and last Six-Day race at MSG,
  202
  and retirement, 108
  and secrets to longevity, 108

Grenda, Alfred, 52–53, 55, 71
Grimm, Willie, 156–157

H

Hamilton, Louis B., 25
Harper, Ted, 159
  and book Six Days of
  Madness, 159
Haverly, Jack, 24
Heid, Jack, 195, 198–199
Hemmingway, Ernest, 50, 58
high-wheel bicycles, 23–27, 38
Hill, Norman, 154, 156–157,
  159, 181
  and Thomas Edison, 154
historic background of Six-Day
  racing, 23–31
Hopkins, Victor, 74, 93, 119
  and fall, 93
Horan, Harry, 79, 81
Horder, Harris, 60, 62
Householder, Ronnie, 191

I

Ignat, Emile, 157
"Iron Man," as nickname for
  McNamara, 183

J

Jacoby, Bill, 193–195, 198
"Jazz Age," as name for 1920s, 68
Jeffries, James J., "Boilermaker," 28
Jones, Bobby, 170, 173
Joyce, Peggy Hopkins, 62
Juner, Oscar, 187

K

Keirin racing, 208
Kilian, Gustav, 164, 172–173,
  177–179, 189
  and Nazi insignia, 178–179
  and Spencer, 164
Kilpatrick, Colonel John Reed, 147
Kingbay, Keith, 132

"Kings of Sport," photograph,
  170, 173
Koblet, Hugo, 195
Kramer, Frank, 41, 50, 58, 85,
  87, 143–144, 164–169
  and DeFilippo, 164–169
  and Neville, 87
  and Spencer, 143–144

L

Lahr, Bert, 185
Lands, Dave, 71, 80
Lapize, Octave, 55
Larsson, Yver, see Lawson, Iver
Lawson, Gus, 35
Lawson, Iver, 29, 35, 40, 41, 44,
  65, 84
  in Australia, 44
  and massage, 84
League of American Wheelmen
  (LAW), 44, 72
  and professionalism, 44
legislation, to control 6-Day
  racing, 28
Lehigh County Velodrome, 209
LeMond, Greg, 85
Letourner, Alfred, 90, 91, 93,
  153, 155, 184–186,
  190–191, 195, 201–202
  in bunk, 153
  and No. 13, 184–186
  post-war, 201–202
  and speed record, 190–191

M

MacFarland, Floyd, 44, 48–59, 71
  in Australia, 44
  and Berlin Six-Day race, 55
  and Paris Six-Day race, 55
  versus Chapman at Madison
  Square Garden, 55
McNamara, Reggie, 13, 52,
  63–64, 78–81, 122, 139,
  181–183

and accident, 183
and European promoters,
    78–81
and granddaughter, 182
and Hall of Fame, 182
and Pope Pius XI, 81
and retirement, 183
and world travels, 63
Madden, Eddie, 63
Madison Square Garden, 10, 24,
    61, 117, 186–187, 201–205
and celebrities, 61
and kitchen, 114–115, 117
and last Six-Day race, 201–205
track overview (illustration),
    186–187
Magin, Jake, 86
Magnani, Joseph, 199
Martin, "Plugger Bill," 24
massage, 84–90, 190
Mazon, Lucien-George, see
    Petit-Breton, Louis
mechanics, 93–99
Mendel, Harry, 171–175, 189
and Spencer, 173
Mihon, Frank Sr., 41
and wife, 41
Miller, Charlie, 24, 25, 28
Montreal, 1972 Six-Day race,
    206, 209
Moran, Jimmy, 50, 50–51, 56, 58
Moretti, Cesar, 189
motor-paced racing, 36–38
Muenster, post-war Six-Day
    racing, 212–214
Murphy, Charles "Mile a
    Minute," 34, 38
Murphy, Pat, 203–205
Mussolini, Benito, 139

N

National Cycling Association
    (NCA), 44, 55, 72, 145
and Spencer's Outlaws, 145

versus League of American
    Wheelmen (LAW), 44
National Football League, 10
Nazi insignia, displayed by Kilian
    and Vopel, 178–179
Neville, Jack, 85–87
and Kramer, 86
and Spears, 86
Newark Velodrome, 56, 59, 103,
    187
and fire, 193
and summer and winter
    racing, 187
"New Jersey Jammers," 122, 126
Norton, J.P., 17–173
Nothstein, Marty, 208–211
Nutley Velodrome, opening of, 187

O

O'Brien, Pat, 148
O'Connor, Dick, 74–75
Oelkers, Ryan Simes, 210–211
Olmo, Guiseppe, 179, 189
"Outlaws," see also Spencer,
    Willie, 142–145, 162–169, 173

P

Paramount bicycles, 99,
    133–134, 199, see also
    Schwinn Bicycle Company
and Magnani, 199
Paris, see Vélodrome d'Hiver
Pearl Harbor, and American
    involvement in World War
    II, 189
Peden, Doug, 164–167,
    172–173, 189
Peden, William, "Torchy",
    164–167, 172–173, 178,
    181–182, 189
Pesek, Erwin, 193–197
and accident, 196–197
and post-war racing, 193–197
Petit-Breton, Louis

(Lucien-George Mazan), 34,
    40, 55
Petri, Otto, 78, 80
Pillsbury, Art, 102
Pius XI, Pope, 81, 139
and McNamara, 139
Plattner, Oscar, 201
points system, 61–65
Post-War recovery, 193–199
Powell, Dick, 169
primes, 61–62
Prince, John Shillington, "Jack,"
    34, 102
and track construction, 34
prize money, 127
program covers (illustrations), 8,
    11–12, 14, 16–21
Prohibition, 68

R

Ratner, Willie, 172–173
"Red Devil," 190–191
as nickname for Cecil Yates, 190
as title of movie, 191
repairs, see mechanics
Riboli, Tino, 156–157, 169
Rice, Grantland, 34
and Bobby Walthour, Sr., 34
Rich, Peter, 211
and cycling magazines, 211
Rickard, George Lewis, "Tex,"
    43–48, 68, 72, 74, 147, 173
as boxing promoter, 72
and death of, 147
and "Kings of Sport"
    photograph, 173
and Madison Square Garden,
    68, 74
Rickenbacker, Eddie, 191
road racing, 10, 13
Robinson, Brian, 201
Rodman, Jerry, 159, 173, 190
Root, Eddie, 56–57, 78
as McNamara's mentor, 78

Root, Florence, "Flossie", 64
Runyon, Damon, 107–111, 114
  and food, 114
Ruth, Babe, 68, 170, 173
  and earnings, 68
Rutt, Walter, 51–52, 55–56

S

Schock, Albert, 24
Schwinn, Ignaz, 99, 190
Schwinn Bicycle Company, 99,
  133–134, 190, 198–199
Simes, Jack II, 208
Simes, Jack III, 208–210
Six Days of Madness, book, 159
Smith, Ted, 203
Spears, Bob, 56, 86
  and Kramer, 86
Spencer, Arthur, 143, 144
Spencer, Freddie, 74–75, 78, 119,
  122, 128, 156–157
  and tobacco advertising, 78
Spencer, Willie, 173
  and "Outlaws," 142–145,
  162-169
stationery (illustrations), 20
Stein, Charley, 114
Stiller, Al, 198
strychnine, 87

T

Taylor, Marshall, "Major," 29, 44
Terront, Charles, 24–25
Thistle Bicycle Company,
  44–45
Thomas, Bobby, 168–169
Thurber, James, 107–111
tickets (illustrations), 19
Tilden, Bill, 170, 173
tobacco advertising, 78, 155
"Torchy," see Peden, William
Tour de France, 10
track construction, 101–105

track racing, compared to road
  racing, 13
trainers, 83–93
training rides, 74, 78, 164
Tunney, Gene, 170, 173
two-rider teams, introduction
  of, 28

U

United States Cycling
  Federation (USCF), 208,
  211
United States Professional
  Racing Organization,
  USPRO, 209
USA Cycling, 209

V

Vallee, Rudy, 151
Vande Velde, John, 208–211
Van Gent, Chris, 195
Van Kempen, Piet, 156–157,
  160, 164
Van Vliet, Arie, 189
Vélodrome d'Hiver, "Vel d'Hiv,"
  50, 54–55, 58
Vélodrome Farm, 173
Vopel, Heinz, 164, 172–173,
  177–179, 189
  and Nazi insignia, 178–179
  and Spencer, 164

W

Walker, Cecil, 74–75, 88–89, 161
  and bike shop Cecil Walker
  Cycles, 161
Walthour, Bobby III, 109–110,
  127
  as child with Bobby II,
  124–125
  and Goullet, 109–110
  and meeting President

Coolidge, 127
Walthour, Bobby IV
  and McNamara accident, 183
Walthour, Bobby Jr., 13, 64,
  74–75, 119–129, 155, 183,
  187, 205
  and last Six-Day race at
  Madison Square Garden,
  205
  and beginning of career, 64
  and MGM, 187
  and tobacco advertising, 155
  with son Bobby III, 124–125
Walthour, Bobby Sr., 13, 33–38,
  43–44, 55
  and Daisy, 43–44
  and earnings, 34
  with family, 37
Walthour, Jimmy Jr., 131–135,
  173, 189
  and divorce, 189
  and earnings, 135
  and marriage, 135
  and vaudeville stage, 132
Wastyn, Emile, 99
Wastyn, Oscar, 96, 98–100
  and bike shop Oscar Wastyn
  Cycles, 96, 99
Weissmuller, Johnny, 170, 173
White Sox, baseball team,
  137–138
Wiley, George, 55
Wilhelm II, German Emperor, 50
Winter, Charlie, 66, 73, 119,
  170, 172–173
Wissel, Ewald, 183
World War II, American
  involvement in, 189

Y

Yaccino, Charley, 193, 198
Yates, Cecil, 181–182, 189–190,
  193